HARD LABOUR

Stress, ill-health and hazardous employment practices

LONDON HAZARDS CENTRE

A London Hazards Centre Handbook

ASTON UNIVERSITY

LIBRARY & INFORMATION SERVICES

Aston Triangle
Birmingham
B4 7ET   Tel: 0121 359 3611
England   Fax: 0121 359 7358

ACKNOWLEDGEMENTS

This book was written as a result of a collaborative effort by Maggie Alexander, Sheila Cohen, Hugh MacGrillen and Fiona Murie. Many others contributed by collecting and passing on information, by assessing the manuscript and by offering advice. I would like to thank Mick Holder, Mike Merritt and Chris Whitehouse, from the London Hazards Centre, Professor Cary Cooper from the University of Manchester Institute of Science and Technology and the many officials and lay members of local and national trade union organisations, who took the time and trouble to assist us.

Thanks are also due to those who have contributed information about their experiences of facing, and tackling, workplace stress. In particular, we are grateful to Christopher Johnstone and Raj Kumar for telling their stories.

This book is dedicated to them, and to all other workers whose health is at risk from stress at work.

Maggie Alexander
London Hazards Centre
August 1994

CONTENTS

1

INTRODUCTION

WORKING HARD

Workers today do not need to be told that work is getting harder — in every sense. The trend in manufacturing towards techniques of 'lean production' just-in-time working, constant improvement, total quality management and so forth — is just the sharpest end in an overall process of **intensification** of labour through which industry, not just in Britain but worldwide, is trying to revive flagging profits. And it does not stop at the borders of private production. The public sector, too, since the emergence of the philosophy of 'market forces', has become influenced by the same rationale that has seen work increasingly contracted out to the private sector and, even where this has been avoided, subjected to the same pressures of reduced workforces and 'flexible' working practices.

These trends in employment — and the unemployment, part-time working, temporary working and general casualisation of the workforce that go along with them — are not usually seen as health and safety issues. Rightly, they are looked on as undermining the basic right of the worker to secure, reasonably paid, rewarding and dignified labour, i.e. fundamentally affecting the terms and conditions of work. The changes in the nature of work and the labour market examined in this handbook do all that and more. But beyond that, as we show here, they also have far-reaching effects on **health and safety**.

Health and safety is not just about hazardous substances like chemicals and asbestos, or dangerous working conditions like those too often found in industries like construction. It is also about the **organisation** of work — the way jobs are designed, the amount of control workers have over them, the speed of work and the length of time spent doing it. It is about pressure put on workers to produce so that they cut corners — and a lack of job security

1

which forces workers to accept unsafe procedures because, if they do not, someone else will. It is about the 'Twenty-Four Hour Society' which forces workers into shifts and exhausting working patterns designed for robots rather than human beings (Moore-Ede 1993). The end result of these practices is the condition known as stress.

LABOUR MARKET CHANGES

Of course, for most people work has never been a soft option. But over the years of fighting for workers' rights, a body of law was established which at least gave some protection from the worst excesses of the 'bad old days'. The Factories Acts, for example, laid the foundations of the safety legislation later brought together and expanded under the 1974 Health and Safety at Work (HSW) Act. Wages Councils were set up to provide a minimum wage for those in the most exploited industries.

More recently, particularly in the years after the second world war, welfare provision such as the National Health Service and social security was matched in the world of work by laws like the Redundancy Payments Act, Employment Protection Act and Trade Union and Labour Rights Act, all passed in the 1960s and early 1970s. These gave workers rights like maternity provision, unfair dismissal protection and standardised payment for job loss.

It was not paradise, just a reasonable basis for workers to have a chance to organise effectively around their interests at work. However, the period since the late 1970s has seen a sharp decline in this trend towards redressing the balance at work — not only in Britain but across the 'advanced' industrial world — as governments have swung away from state provision and towards the unleashing of 'market forces'. This has not just meant the clawing back of much of the legal protection mentioned here — an issue we come back to under the heading of 'Deregulation' — it has also gone alongside massive changes in the whole nature of work and of the labour market which, taken together, seem to be forcing workers across Europe back to what the GMB has called 'the reincarnation of 19th-century working conditions' (GMB 1993).

From 'core' to 'periphery'

Over the past ten to fifteen years, the limited stability and acceptance of worker rights gained during the post-war 'boom' have been ruthlessly undermined as employers have moved to a profit-driven assault on job security, pay and working conditions. Increasingly, the pattern has moved from what has been called 'core' employment — stable, full-time, permanent jobs which workers can reasonably assume will continue with the same employer — to a 'periphery' of part-time, temporary, casualised workers ready to move around the labour market at the bidding of the employer.

All these changed types of employment — termed by the European Commission 'non-standard' or 'atypical' — have been on the increase in the past couple of decades. A recent Labour Research Department pamphlet shows that part-time working has increased from 18.2 per cent of all UK employees in June 1971 to 25.6 per cent in June 1991, with the growth particularly high in sectors like retailing (Labour Research Department 1992). In other areas of service work, like banking, employees have been forced to switch to part-time hours when they would have preferred to work full-time. And even traditional manufacturing work like car assembly has seen the increased introduction of workers on fixed-term contracts, along with 'outsourcing' of many areas of work previously carried out in-plant.

'So what?' you may say. Part-time or temporary working may not be good news for my pay or conditions, but it does not affect my health. But if you said that, you would be wrong. The move to an increasingly casualised workforce has three main implications for health and safety:

▲ loss of organisation at work. 'Peripheral' workers are not, on the whole, unionised workers. And health and safety, as we see later on, depends crucially on effective organisation where it most matters — in the workplace.
▲ a general culture where safety, if considered at all, has a price on its head. Sir John Cullen, Chair of the Health and Safety Commission (HSC) said in 1989, after the Piper Alpha, Kings Cross and Zeebrugge ferry disasters: *'the enterprise culture, the opening up of markets, and the need to survive competition place businesses under unprecedented pressure which means that increasing numbers of people — the public as well as employees — are potentially at risk.'*

3

▲ direct impact on the workers involved in terms of **stress**. Job insecurity, lack of control over work — even more common in 'peripheral' forms of employment — and the low pay which goes along with this have all been shown to contribute massively to the health and safety issue of the 1990s — stress at work.

Casual work is not easy work. Homeworking, for example, one of Britain's growing industries, means long hours of intensive labour, often in unsafe conditions, at exploitative rates of pay. A recent report estimates that over a million workers, 90 per cent of them women, do paid work at home (National Group on Homeworking 1990).

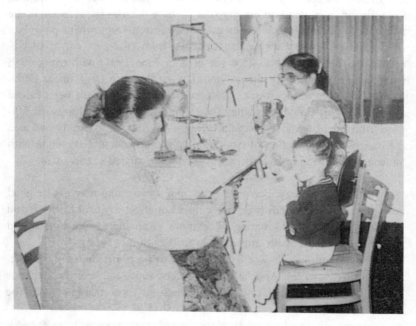

As well as the stress of low-paid, intensive labour, homeworkers and their children may be exposed to hazards from equipment, chemicals and dust.   *London Hazards Centre*

It seems that the strongest motive for the move to part-time employment, side by side with the obvious saving in labour costs, is flexibility. A number of studies have shown that, particularly in the retail sector, employers are pacing their employment patterns to follow closely peaks and troughs in demand. The most common example is in the large chain stores, where part-time workers are employed on a morning and afternoon shift basis, overlapping at lunchtime when the shops are at their busiest. About a third of all retail staff are now estimated to be part-time.

Large hotel chains often gauge their demand for worker hours on the basis of seasonal factors and the time of the week. But these new patterns can also be found in the public sector, where local authorities, for example, employ between them over 800,000 part-time workers. A representative from the Local Government Management Board, which oversees the councils' terms and conditions, argued that: *'We need part-timers. You need catering staff at lunch-time in schools, not all day.'*

This kind of approach has by now resulted in a number of cases of employers directly reducing the hours of their own workforces from full- to part-time, a trend again most common in the retail sector. At Burton's clothes shops, for example, a reorganisation of work in early 1993 led to the shedding of 2,000 full-time jobs and their replacement with about 3,000 part-time posts. Other big retailers, such as BHS and the Allied Maples Group, have now taken similar steps, followed most recently by the Sock Shop, which in January 1994 announced its decision to switch its 400 staff from full-time to 20-hour, three-day part-time contracts.

PRIVATISATION

Homeworking is one of the most extreme forms of casualised work. But throughout the economies of Britain and Europe the trend towards this kind of peripheral, deregulated employment has been made worse by another kind of pressure — privatisation.

During the postwar years of relative growth and stability, governments were in the forefront of setting acceptable standards for industry and employment. Council workers, for example, have traditionally enjoyed much higher levels of health and safety control, particularly in construction, than those in the private sector. But now even this basic level of acceptance of the need for regulation has come under increasing threat from the privatisation, contracting-out and deregulation of vast swathes of the public sector leading to a deterioration in health and safety standards for workers.

British Gas, British Airways, British Telecom, Girobank, Rolls-Royce, the water authorities, the electricity industry and many others have come under the auctioneer's hammer during the 1980s and 1990s — with consequent massive pressure on jobs, pay and working conditions. Shortly after British Telecom was privatised in 1984, a damning report was issued in which BT was condemned for 'barely adequate' and 'deteriorating' safety standards since privatisation *(Health and Safety at Work* July 1987). The report showed how pressure of work, fears about job security and poor management practices had led to shortcuts and the abandonment of safety rules strictly adhered to before privatisation.

The same record is threatened in industries being 'groomed for privatisation' like British Rail. A 1993 Health and Safety Commission report on British Rail privatisation has already warned of the *'clear safety implications arising from government proposals for privatising the railways'* — for example, through an influx of new managers who *'may have limited experience of railway safety'* *(Hazards* 1993). As one former BR senior operations manager put it, *'A fragmented railway is a less safe railway'*.

COMPETITIVE TENDERING AND CONTRACTING OUT

But, although the privatisation programme continues apace, industries do not have to be sold off wholesale for workers to experience the privatisation of their jobs with all the ensuing attacks on working conditions. Since the mid-1980s, the government has enacted a policy of **compulsory competitive tendering** which has pushed huge sectors of local authority and health service workers into competing with — if not being directly taken over by — the private sector.

The contracting-out process in the public sector has most recently been extended to the Civil Service, where 'market testing' of the various government departments has put workers under increasing pressure. The kind of intensified working practices civil service workers are subjected to in an atmosphere of intensified competition was illustrated by the case of keyboard operator Kathleen Harris, who recently won a landmark compensation case for repetitive strain injury (RSI). Before her enforced retirement from a London tax office in summer 1993, Mrs Harris was expected to average four key strokes a second and worked a seven-and-a-half-hour day with no breaks apart from half an hour for lunch. The permanent injuries to her arm were said to be due as much to the bad working environment as to the speed of work — while her union, the Inland Revenue Staff Federation (IRSF), pointed out that a 'growing army' of RSI sufferers, mainly low-paid women workers, is being created by the management tendency to 'crack whips' in an attempt to improve productivity (*Independent* 20 January 1994).

DEREGULATION

Privatisation of jobs does not end with competitive tendering. Large areas of the public sector are also being 'deregulated' or privatised in other back-door ways. London Underground (LUL), for example, while still nominally in the public sector, recently contracted out some of its track work — with fatal results. Three London Underground workers and one contractor were killed in an accident at Chorleywood in May 1990 after railway line work was done by non-LUL workers for the first time.

The same pattern is echoed in the bus industry, where deregulation has led not only to slashed pay rates for bus workers but also dangerously long working hours — highlighted by the Transport and General Workers' Union (TGWU) in their leaflet *Is Your Driver Safe?* — and massively increased driver stress. Quotes from drivers in a GLC video, made shortly after One-Person Operation (OPO) of buses was introduced, included: '*I literally used to shake like a leaf at the end of the day. OPO driving will kill someone before much longer*' (ex-OPO driver) and: '*Sometimes he says he needs to explode to offload the pressure. He gets this gripping feeling in his stomach*' (OPO driver's wife).

In addition to deregulation in selected industries, the Health and Safety Commission is in the process of reviewing all health and safety laws with the intention of 'lifting the burden of red tape' from industry. It plans to reduce the volume of health and safety law by as much as 40 per cent over a period of time (Health and Safety Commission 1994).

'FLEXIBILITY' EQUALS 'INTENSITY' OF LABOUR

The re-organisation of employment, along lines of 'freedom', labour-market deregulation and so on, has not been good news for workers. Just as basic pay and conditions have been abandoned to market forces, so has any humane concern for workers' lives and health. But, under the intense competitive pressures of today's industry, even workers in the so-called 'core' sector — those with full-time and at least nominally permanent jobs — are far from immune to intensified working processes which increasingly threaten their physical and mental well-being.

Perhaps the best-known of these processes comes under the umbrella of what is ironically known as 'lean production', an idea explained below.

'Eight-hour aerobics'

Earlier in this introduction, we spoke about the way in which employers are now pushing workers in and out of the labour force, into part-time, temporary and contract work, in order to suit their own need for flexible production. As one report put it, *'Flexibility has become a buzz word for management ... and has been referred to as 'the key concept of the 1980s'* (Centre for Alternative Industrial and Technological Systems 1986). A distinction has been made, however, between the *numerical* flexibility of the labour force represented in the kind of labour market changes discussed above, and what has been called *functional* flexibility — management-ordained changes in the organisation of work itself. Clearly, this kind of flexibility will affect even full-time workers in apparently secure jobs.

'Functional' flexibility usually contains some or all of the following elements:
▲ abolition of clear divisions of labour or demarcation
▲ introduction of multi-skilling often without adequate training
▲ changes in pay and grading structures

▲ changes in training from a 'trade' to a 'task' basis
▲ extension of work from direct to indirect (e.g. line workers to carry out janitor functions).

> An attempt at functional flexibility led to an industrial dispute at the National Association of Citizens Advice Bureaux in Spring 1994 after skilled printers were asked to take on porterage tasks for which no training had been offered. At the time of writing, the dispute was still unresolved.

Many of these management strategies foreshadowed the more complete, worked-out management techniques now being introduced under the umbrella term of 'lean production'. ('Japanisation' is a term that has also been used for these techniques, but can be seen as suspect because it suggests that Japanese *people*, not just managers, are responsible!) 'Lean production' takes the principles involved in *both* 'numerical' and 'functional' flexibility further and faster — with drastic consequences for workers.

Included in this package of new management techniques are:
▲ **'just-in-time'** production. This means stocks are kept to their lowest possible level, eliminating the 'cushioning' provided by the traditional 'just-in-case' stock buffer system. While this makes sense in engineering terms, in practice it means weak spots in the production process have to be immediately dealt with by the workers involved, putting them under intensified pressure.
▲ **'constant improvement'** (Japanese term — kaizen) stems from and is linked with just-in-time in that the smallest number of workers possible is assigned to each job, under very strict, 'lean' methods of production. As soon as it is shown that a job can be done with this number, pressure is put on to speed up work and reduce the numbers — hence constant improvement.
▲ **teamworking**. This is perhaps the best known of the new techniques — and the one that seems most attractive. Instead of stringing workers out along a traditional assembly line, they are reorganised into 'teams' to carry out specific group tasks, each with a 'team leader'. Unfortunately, instead of involving workers creatively in planning and controlling their own work

organisation, *'the tendency is in the opposite direction — to specify every move a worker makes in far greater detail than ever before...Workers who are brought onto the team are expected to follow detailed procedures that have been worked over and over to eliminate free time and which specify how each motion is to be carried out'* (*Labour Notes* 1988). In fact the whole rationale of 'teams' is not to give workers greater input, but to undermine the strength of union organisation in the workplace by promoting the myth that worker and management interests are all of a piece. 'Team leaders' are substituted for shop stewards, and the whole 'team concept' ideology promotes the notion of common goals which do not need any independent worker representation.

▲ **quality circles**. This is another well-known 'Japanese' management approach which had workers lining up and doing early-morning exercises, then getting together into discussion groups (time unpaid) to produce ideas for improving quality. In fact quality circles have now been dropped by a lot of British firms, but the idea keeps popping up with new Japanese 'inward investment' companies.

▲ **'total quality management'** (TQM). This is perhaps one of the most loaded of these management approaches in terms of its brainwashing potential — and jargon! The idea is that every organisation is 'in pursuit of excellence' (the title of an early management 'guru' book on these lines) and that the 'customer' comes first. Fellow-workers are also termed customers and the idea is to put their needs before yours — in other words hurry production up the line!

The implications for health and safety of this kind of intense pressure are clear. An ex-supervisor at a Nissan plant recalls, *'We hired exceptionally good people, people we thought we could keep for the rest of their working lives. I ran into one of them at the pharmacy the other day. He looked like he was dead. He's lost 30 pounds, he's had a shoulder operation, and now he's taking medication for his hand. He said to me, "I think they've got us on a four- or five-year cycle. They'll wear us out and then hire new blood.' I think he may be right."'*

Service work is not safe either

Of course, in talking about these new techniques for squeezing an ever-increasing amount of 'hard labour' out of workers, the emphasis has mainly been on manufacturing. But, as we all know, the trend in production generally — one also reflected in the shift to part-time, temporary, casual kinds of employment as described above — is a shift *away* from manufacturing towards the service sector.

Tim Nuttall

On the surface, this looks like good news on the health and safety front. The 1993 Health and Safety Commission Annual Report showed the number of deaths at work for 1992-3 as the lowest on record, for the third year running — and this decrease is widely attributed to the decline in heavy manufacturing industry (Health and Safety Commission 1993). What the figures do not emphasise, though, is the correspondingly greater rise in accidents and injuries to service workers. The 1991-2 Health and Safety Commission Report on Health and Safety in Service Industries provides a damning indictment of the situation in this sector with phrases like: *'During the past six years the rate of over-3-day injuries has risen substantially in all main industries of the local authority sector* [ie. retail, hotel and catering, and leisure and recreation — industries which now come under local authority supervision on health and safety]. *This appears to reflect worsening performance rather than better reporting of injuries.'* The report adds that *'work in retail, wholesale and hotel industries has over four-fifths of the accident rate in manufacturing as a whole.'*

Horrific examples of fatalities and injuries given in the report for this sector include a number of cases where 'rushing' and pressure of work had contributed to the accident. For example, a woman working in a warehouse was killed when boxes of goods weighing five tonnes collapsed on to her — the warehouse manager knew the boxes had not been stacked properly, but had not had time to rectify the problem.

STRESS — THE HAZARD OF THE NINETIES

Stress at work emerged as one of the leading elements in a recent survey of work-related illnesses carried out by the Health and Safety Executive as a 'footnote' to the 1990 Labour Force Survey. While the growing phenomenon of repetitive strain injury (RSI) accounted for some 50,000 self-reported injuries, stress and depression accounted for a further 183,000 cases. A recent survey of absenteeism carried out by the Industrial Society pinpointed stress as the second highest cause of time off for sickness (*Engineer* 1993).

Of course, 'stress' *may* be seen as a highly individual factor — 'different people react to pressure in different ways', etc. However, a significant body of scientific opinion backs up the view that stress *must* be taken seriously as a health and safety issue. Professor Tom Cox, author of a recent report on occupational stress commissioned by the Health and Safety Executive, has argued that a 'control cycle', as required by existing legislation, should be developed as part of a more structured approach to the problem of stress at work (Cox 1993).

Along similar lines, Professor Cary Cooper, an expert on stress in the workplace, states that *'It is now recognised that the way a job is designed or the way people are managed can affect their health and well-being as much as exposing them to a bit of machinery or a toxin.'*

In Part 2, we explore in detail the symptoms, effects and causes of workplace stress. In the next section we look at some of the changes in employment practice that have taken place over the past decade and that have contributed significantly to the creation of stress in the workplace.

Low control, long hours

While four million workers in Britain kick their heels on the dole, millions of others are forced into working weeks far exceeding any safe limit — because their basic pay rates are so low they have no choice but to put in long hours of overtime. Or because, like seafarers after the imposition by P&O of 24-hour shifts in 1986, they are given no choice. Or because 'anti-social' shift patterns are integrated into the whole system of production. The safety implications are well known — though seldom well publicised. Three major cases stand out — the Clapham rail disaster, the sinking of the 'Herald of Free Enterprise' and the 1990 M42 pile-up in which six people died. In all these cases and many more, massive tragedies occurred because the workers involved were subjected to inhuman working schedules. The Clapham rail crash, in which 35 people were killed, was allegedly caused by faulty work done by a technician who had taken only one day off in the previous 13 weeks. Signalling technicians in the department routinely worked seven-day weeks and frequently went for 13 hours with only a five-minute break.

A number of studies have pointed out just how bad shiftworking is for health. A Confederation of Health Service Employees (COHSE) study carried out in the wake of a Health and Safety Executive report on shiftworking shows that nervous disorders such as anxiety and depression are more common amongst shiftworkers, that they suffer more digestive disorders and ulcers, due both to increased stress and irregular mealtimes, and are 40 per cent more likely to suffer heart disease than day workers (COHSE 1992). More recently, a British Psychological Society occupational conference held in January 1994 was told by researchers from Heriot-Watt that *'only the hardiest of workers could easily tolerate shiftwork'* (*Financial Times* 4 January 1994).

Terms and conditions for stress

Many factors surrounding the **organisation** of work, therefore — pace, pressure, the sheer amount of work in terms of hours and shifts — contribute both to work-related accidents and to a whole range of work-related illnesses, particularly stress. But finally, it has been shown that even the basic **terms and conditions** of work — issues like pay, sickness benefit, disciplinary procedures and so on — can affect workers' well-being. Restrictive trade union regulations, deregulation, casualisation, payment-by-results and fear of redundancy all seem to be adding to the levels of stress. The political and economic climate cannot be divorced from health effects.

All these problems are exacerbated by **pay systems** that act on a 'work harder — earn more' basis. But in non-manual sectors, the trend towards systems like performance-related pay is taking a toll on workers' well-being, leading to growing problems like repetitive strain injury (RSI). Productivity schemes, performance-related pay, bonus systems and overtime incentives, all payment systems that are based on piece rates tend to increase the rate of RSI by encouraging the worker to work as long as possible as fast as possible.

Job insecurity and the related disciplinary systems growing up in many firms are a major contributory factor to stress at work. Apart from the obvious pressure in industries like construction that if you will not do an unsafe job someone out there will, fear of redundancy in itself is a potent force raising stress and anxiety levels.

Fear of losing the job may push workers not only into working long hours — itself bad for their health — but into coming into work even when sick, a tendency made worse by the recent government deregulation of **sick-pay schemes**. The Statutory Sick Pay Act, which came into force in April 1994, abolishes the 80 per cent reimbursement of employers' statutory sick pay costs, although some small employers are excepted. Clearly, this has the effect of making employers exert stricter discipline on 'absenteeism'. A recent *Hazards* report shows that closer policing of absentees leads to lower levels of sickness absence — even when workers *should* be at home (*Hazards* 1993). A NALGO branch secretary quoted in the article gives an example: '*One man in the building section had an industrial injury — he came back to work when he recovered and sustained another injury and took time off to recover. A sickness monitoring meeting decided to sack him despite the fact that the doctor had signed him off. He has now taken retirement on the grounds of ill-health.*'

Such considerations have not stopped the UK from eagerly competing in the international market as purveyors of the lowest-paid and most 'flexible' workforce. Cases like the transfer of production from Hoover's Dijon plant to Cambuslang in Scotland through the undercutting of French pay and conditions provide shameful examples of this 'bidding-down' strategy. In a reverse example of this trend, transfer of production by the Timex Corporation in 1993 from Dundee to the far East, following on a courageous battle by its Scottish workforce against attacks on their pay and conditions, demonstrates the formidable power of multinational corporations to abandon traditionally well-organised labour markets for the super-exploitation of the Third World.

Ironically, the recent Rover sale to BMW on the basis of the much-trumpeted 'turnaround' achieved in the company at its workers' expense was completed in the wake of union agreement to a Company Plan which promised, in return for massive increases in flexibility and pace of working, the prized goal of a 'Job For Life'.

Just how meaningless this is has been shown by the accounts of workers at Rover's Cowley plant, who describe how an increasing number of workers on temporary, fixed-term contracts are in fact being hired by the company to cope with fluctuations in demand. In addition, the company's absenteeism, lateness and sickness provisions have now become so draconian that workers risk losing their jobs with only the most minor infringements of a total attendance pattern. For example, three separate sickness absences, or five episodes of lateness in one year, will slot a worker into the first stage of the disciplinary procedure, threatening them eventually with the sack. Yet repeated sickness and lateness are symptomatic of stress caused by this kind of system of employment.

The use of annualised or even 'zero' hours programmes is an example of this approach. Under annualised hours, workers' contracts are changed so that they agree to work a certain number of hours a year, rather than any fixed pattern per day or week. This gives employers total flexibility to require, for example, workers to carry out a 14-hour shift if a crisis crops up in the plant, with their only compensation extra time off in lieu — a 'privilege' often difficult for workers in low-wage, exhausting jobs to use constructively.

As the following story shows, even those working in the very organisations responsible for promoting improvements in the nation's health are not immune from the kind of work practices guaranteed to cause stress.

'We have contracts which require us to do a minimum of 36 hours a week. In practice, the workload is such that most of the workers in the department do up to 55 a week just to get through the most urgent jobs. Any 'overtime' we do is unpaid, and we can only take time off in lieu of extra hours done at the weekend, before 8.00 in the morning, or after 7.00pm at night. This shows that only work done on top of this eleven-hour day is perceived as extra. Added to the pressure caused by the sheer volume of work, part of our holiday and pay entitlement is performance-related. The unrealistic workloads mean that you have to be achieving maximum productivity all the time to have any prospect of receiving performance-related pay or holiday. The employers rely on the dedication and commitment of the staff to stop this whole system from falling apart at the seams. But I do not know how long this can last. I feel frustrated and angry — partly because of the pressure I'm under, and partly because the way the work is structured means that I rarely have the chance to do the job to the best of my ability. After several sleepless nights, often waking at one or two in the morning worrying about how to solve a problem at work, I'm unable to work in the most effective way. Lots of us in the Department come into work even when we're sick — partly because you run the risk of being called in for a 'counselling' interview if you're off for a couple of days, and partly because the work just piles up to an even more unmanageable level when you're away.' Health Promotion Adviser for a London Health Authority.

In some TV companies this policy has been carried to extremes, with workers required to work shifts as long as 70 hours at short notice. While they may receive weeks of free time in return, the pattern is never predictable, making it impossible to plan leisure activities and totally ruling out workable childcare arrangements. Such developments show that even relatively skilled, professional employees are not immune to the demands of the 'flexibility' drive. Contracts specifying 'zero' hours, on the other hand, tend to affect much lower-skilled employees. In these agreements workers like supermarket shelf-fillers are employed on a basis of no specified hours, but are expected to be 'on call' whenever extra demand requires. Recent job advertisements for building labourers, for example, specify that such workers should have their own phone at home so that they can be called to jobs at short notice.

Such increasingly privatised, individualised working arrangements — sometimes spelt out in the form of 'individual' or 'personal' employment contracts — are becoming a feature of what is described as new 'high-tech' forms of homeworking. Computer-based work such as data inputting or word processing, and an increasing range of telecommunications jobs, can now be carried out directly from home or by an individual worker 'on the move', linked to the employer through a computer modem. Some employers have been able to save up to £3,000 per worker by instituting these methods.

Such forms of work organisation allow for a high degree of monitoring and are a long way from the romantic 'high-tech cottage' dreamt up by some 'flexible specialisation' theorists in the more optimistic 1980s. A recent *Guardian* report gives a vivid, if depressing, picture of the everyday conditions of one such worker:

> *'For the forefront of technological revolution, Sharon Curtis' back bedroom looks a bit of a mess. Toys, books and the innumerable pieces of junk that a family accumulates just about crowd out the battered Amstrad and printer that are the tools of her trade. It is about as far from the image of the teleworker communicating electronically from a far-flung croft as can be imagined. Mrs Curtis works from a street in north London, collecting work and delivering typed letters and scripts in an old banger...with two children, she and her husband Ray, a postman, find her income essential.' (Guardian 22 March 1994).*

JOB INSECURITY IS BAD FOR YOUR HEALTH

First of all, a casualised job is unlikely to be an organised job. The sharp decline in trade unionism from 58 per cent of the workforce in unions in 1980 to 40 per cent today has almost entirely encompassed the 'new' service sector employment areas where these jobs are concentrated. In an unorganised workplace, you do not have the chance to stand up for your rights or to have a say in how your place of work is run. Low-margin employers like sub-contractors are unlikely to be too conscientious when it comes to implementing every detail of even inadequate health and safety provision.

Along with this lack of union organisation — which, for example, prevents workers from taking advantage of legal provisions for electing health and safety representatives — goes the very lack of job security itself, which means workers are far less likely to protest against unsafe corner-cutting working practices for fear of losing their jobs. A supreme example of this is in the construction industry, where the carnage on the building sites continues on the basis of 'If you won't do it, someone else will'. But examples like the one given above on the Rover disciplinary procedure are evidence of a growing trend in which workers, even if they are injured or otherwise ill, are afraid to be sick for fear of losing their jobs. Ironically, this obsession with cranking up attendance patterns is now registering among the more 'caring' professions of the public sector, with employees being offered 'counselling' (a disguised form of disciplinary process) if their sickness absence exceeds certain levels.

So job insecurity is a potent force for weakening workers' organisation, confidence and ability to speak up for themselves at work. But more than that — and this is our second point — this kind of casual, peripheral employment has in itself been found to have a serious effect on the health of those involved.

A study published in March 1994, which brought together the work of a team of academics based on interviews with 6,000 employed and unemployed people, has established a close link between psychological well-being and individuals' sense of job security — or lack of it (Burchell 1994). The new tier of insecure labour created by the government's much-vaunted 'flexibility', the study concludes, is damaging health, creating depression, causing marriage breakdown and leading to an increased sense of social isolation.

Unemployment is only the most acute form of this set of social problems, which is also linked to a increased degree of **underemployment** in which people find themselves shifting in and out of the labour market in unstable, part-time, poorly-paid jobs. Both unemployed men and those in low-paid insecure jobs were found to suffer roughly the same levels of depression, isolation and ill-health stemming from their situation. The stress resulting from job insecurity was also found to be a major factor in marriage breakdown.

So today's 'peripheral' labour market does not only lower pay, weaken union organisation, intensify labour and create the conditions for unsafe, unhealthy workplaces — it also attacks workers themselves, as people, at the heart of their physical and mental well-being.

Finally, workers are extensively — and increasingly — affected by **violence** in their working lives — an issue we examine in Part 2. The overall climate of recession and 'underemployment' pushes workers into taking jobs as, for example, security guards which combine long hours and low pay with solitary working, thus inevitably raising the risk of serious violence — and the stress that accompanies that risk. The introduction of systems like One-Person Operation (OPO) on the buses leave drivers alone on 24 hour schedules to face the common hazard of drunken and abusive passengers. In general, the ever-tightening staffing levels imposed by cost-conscious employers leave workers increasingly vulnerable to attacks — for example by mentally ill patients in under-resourced, poorly staffed hospitals.

EUROPE TO THE RESCUE?

The picture we have painted of today's deteriorating working conditions, and their effects on workers' health and safety, is a grim one — though, we are afraid, only too accurate. This does not mean we lack ideas for strategies or solutions — we are saving those for Part 3! But many trade unionists, anxious about the increasing threat to health and safety provision — as well as general terms and conditions — have been looking to Europe for an answer.

There are good reasons for looking in this direction. The **Social Charter** (now Chapter) adopted by the European Council in December 1989, lays the basis for a comprehensive programme of workers' rights aimed at providing a level playing field of harmonised conditions across the whole

European Community (EC — now known as EU or European Union). The Social Charter included:

▲ freedom of movement for labour including equal access to employment and social benefits
▲ improvement of living and working conditions, especially for part-time and temporary ('atypical') workers
▲ the right of equal treatment for men and women
▲ the right to freedom of association and free collective bargaining
▲ the right to workplace health protection and safety, including training, information and participation for employees.

The UK, already suspicious of the whole European project, adopted a systematic policy of 'opt-out' which reached its culmination in late 1991 when Britain was the only one of the 12 EC states not to agree the Social Chapter of the Maastricht Treaty.

A major example of the British government's reluctance to co-operate in any European project to establish minimal worker rights is its attitude to hours of work, about which Sir John Cullen, Chair of the Health and Safety Commission has argued: *'there is no good evidence to suggest that they have any effect on health and safety'*, (*Health and Safety at Work* 1991).

Britain is the only EC member state to have almost no regulation of the hours of the working week, overtime, nightwork or holidays. As a result, UK employees work longer hours than any of their European counterparts — an average of 43.7 a week, compared with the European average of 40.4 hours. Almost 30 per cent of British workers work over 46 hours a week — more than in any other European country (*Labour Research* 1994).

WHAT IS TO BE DONE?

In his introduction to the GMB's anti-deregulation *Freedom to Kill* pamphlet, the General Secretary, John Edmonds, argues that *'Work should enhance life; it should not endanger health.'* In Britain today, we are a very long way from that ideal.

An appalling toll on workers' lives, a rising level of work-related illnesses, a government set on demolishing what legal defences workers still have, may make people feel powerless in the face of the onslaught. But there are strategies and resources available to workers to defend and extend their rights on health and safety and these are examined in this handbook which we hope will be useful to all those trying to combat workplace stress.

2

STRESS AND HEALTH

'Excessive stress can effectively destroy the quality of life for the individual, his or her family and for society as a whole. It has become as dangerous as pollution to modern society' (Clive Purkis, Director of the European Foundation for the Improvement of Living and Working Conditions, 1993).

In this part we look at the effects on health of stress at work. We present evidence to dispel the idea that stress is exclusively a condition suffered by middle-aged male managers and we offer some ideas for counteracting the kinds of work organisation which lead inevitably to work-related stress.

FINANCIAL FACTS

Let's start with some bald economic statistics. The total annual cost to the country of work-related accidents and ill-health is estimated by the HSE to be between £11 *billion* and £16 *billion* (Davies and Teasdale 1994). £7 billion of this total is accounted for by workforce stress (Rochez and Scoggins 1993). According to the HSE's research, almost 10 per cent of the entire workforce suffers from work-related stress at any one time (Davies and Teasdale 1994) and 80 million working days are lost each year due to mental illness (CBI 1993). However, a Europe-wide survey by the European Commission in 1991-2 suggests that this figure may be a gross underestimate. The survey found that almost one in two European employees suffer from occupational stress (European Commission 1992).

These shocking statistics demonstrate that moral, social and ethical considerations are failing to persuade employers to carry out their duty to provide safe systems of work for their employees. Perhaps the HSE's recent advice to employers that accidents and ill-health 'will hurt your balance sheet' will have more impact. Fear of spiralling employee health-care costs and compensation, argues Professor Cary Cooper, a prominent researcher into causes of occupational stress, is the reason why levels of stress-related illnesses are declining in the US but not in the UK where the tax payer, via the National Health Service, picks up the bill (Cooper 1986).

It will be interesting to see whether future statistics bear out the findings of a recent Confederation of British Industry (CBI) survey that 60 per cent of companies now design jobs and training to alleviate stress (CBI 1993). It would be encouraging to believe that UK employers shared CBI Director General Howard Davies' view that '*A company's workforce is its most important asset. An individual's state of health, both mental and physical, is critical to the quality of their work.*' (*Hazards* Winter 1993/4). Unfortunately, the evidence from hazards centres and occupational health projects around the country is that, far from valuing their workforce, the majority of employers see them as an expendable commodity, to be exploited for maximum productivity, then discarded when ill-health threatens to incapacitate them.

Of course, to victims of work-related ill-health and their families the costs go far beyond financial costs and include the loss in overall quality of life and general well-being resulting from the suffering associated with illness, the worry and grief caused to their families and friends, and the effects of long-term or permanent incapacity.

DEFINING STRESS

Stress is the term often used to describe distress, fatigue and feelings of not being able to cope. There are numerous academic definitions (including engineering, physiological and psychological approaches) which focus on the relationship between individuals and their environment, but we have chosen the following definition to encompass the most important elements:

When the demands and pressures placed on individual workers do not match the resources available, or do not meet the individual's needs and motivations, stress can occur and endanger that person's health and well-being. In the short term, stress can be debilitating; in the long term, stress can kill.

Symptoms of work-related stress

Defining a clear link between occupational causes and the resulting symptoms is much harder for a condition such as stress than is it for a disease such as mesothelioma (which is caused only by exposure to asbestos). Because many of the symptoms of stress are generalised — such as increased anxiety or irritability — it is easy for them to be ascribed to a characteristic of the worker, rather than to a condition of the work. As we will show, however, there is mounting scientific and medical evidence that certain types of work and work organisation do have a measurable, and verifiable, impact on the health of workers.

The range of symptoms includes the following:

Physical symptoms
▲ headaches and migraine
▲ colds and other respiratory infections
▲ asthma
▲ raised cholesterol levels
▲ increased blood pressure
▲ ulcers
▲ digestive tract disorders
▲ heart disease
▲ increased risk of cancer
▲ thyroid disorders
▲ diabetes
▲ menstrual disorders
▲ possible effects on pregnancy
▲ sleepless nights
▲ lethargy
▲ karoshi (sudden death from overwork)

Mental health symptoms
▲ irritability
▲ depression
▲ increased risk of suicide
▲ withdrawal

▲ anxiety
▲ low self-esteem
▲ 'burn-out'
▲ post-traumatic stress disorder

Psychosocial symptoms
▲ heavy drinking
▲ increased use of drugs
▲ smoking
▲ eating disorders
▲ increased sickness absence
▲ increased accident rates
▲ breakdown of relationships

Some degree of stress is a normal part of life and provides part of the stimulus to learn and grow, without having an adverse effect on health. When stress is intense, continuous or repeated — as is often the case with occupational stress — ill-health can result.

The experience of stress can affect the way individuals think, feel and behave, and can also cause physiological changes. Many of the short- and long-term illnesses caused by stress can be accounted for by the physiological changes that take place when the body is placed under stress.

EFFECT OF STRESS ON THE BODY

Information on the physiological effects of stress could take up a book on its own. In this section we concentrate on well-documented effects that have been clearly linked to occupational causes.

There are four physiological systems that are particularly vulnerable to stress (Cox 1993): the cardiovascular system (heart and blood circulation system); the endocrine system (the hormone system); the gastrointestinal system (digestive system) and the immune system (the body's defence system).

Fight or flight

The body reacts to stress in the first instance by invoking the flight or fight response. This reaction was very useful to our ancestors — enabling a quick response to threatening situations. But in today's workplace it is often impossible for people to fight the stress or run away.

During the response, the hormone adrenalin is released, increasing heart rate, blood pressure and sweat production. There is an increase in muscle tension, and breathing becomes rapid and shallow. The hormone cortisol is also released, which in turn stimulates the release of body fuels like glucose, fatty acids and amino acids. Intense, prolonged or repeated provocation of this response by having, for example, constantly to meet unrealistic deadlines, causes increased wear and tear on the body, and contributes to what have been called 'diseases of adaptation'.

Research in rats suggests that prolonged exposure to adrenalin and cortisol can accelerate the aging of brain cells and lead to impairment of learning and memory (*Consumer Currents* August 1991).

Heart and blood circulation system

If stress is continuous, permanent high blood pressure or hypertension can develop. This hypertension can damage blood vessels walls and disturb kidney function. It can lead to bursting of blood vessels in the brain (a stroke) and around the heart (a heart attack or coronary), both of which can be fatal.

When stress is continuous, the body has no chance to reabsorb the body fuels released as part of the stress response. Fatty acids build up in the blood stream and fat is deposited in blood vessel walls, causing a narrowing of arteries. The arteries can harden, blood clots form, the supply of oxygen to heart muscle is reduced and pain, known as angina can result. When the oxygen supply to heart muscle is severely restricted, heart attacks, and death, can result.

A recent review of scientific research on this issue reported that 12 out of 14 studies showed that there was a clear link between occupational stress and heart disease (Landsbergis 1993). Furthermore, it was estimated that 23 per cent of heart disease (and 150,000 deaths per year) in the US could potentially be prevented if the stress levels in jobs with the worst stress levels were reduced to the average of other occupations. The studies also showed that more women and black workers faced higher levels of stress than their male, white, counterparts.

In Japan, sudden death from a heart attack or stroke brought on by overwork is known as *karoshi*. Karoshi first emerged as a problem in the 1970s, coinciding with cuts in jobs and a resulting increase in individuals' workloads. Many Japanese bank employees work an average day of 12 hours. As we showed in Part 1, far from learning from these tragedies, the UK boasts of the attractions of its 'deregulated labour market' — a euphemism for a licence to overwork and underpay large sections of the workforce.

Karoshi takes place in Britain as well. In January 1994, junior doctor Alan Massie collapsed and died in Warrington District Hospital at the end of an 86-hour work week (*Observer* 10 April 1994). He had worked seven of the previous eight days including two unbroken spells of 27 hours and one of 24 hours. His death came at a time when the Government claimed that it had introduced a new deal for junior hospital doctors whose working hours were restricted to a maximum of 83 per week in April 1993. However a survey by the British Medical Association in January 1994 found that 1,200 doctors were still working beyond the limit, though this figure is disputed by the Government.

> Chris Johnstone was so alarmed by the extremely long hours, 88 per week, he worked as a junior hospital doctor that he brought an action for personal injury against his employer, Bloomsbury Health Authority, in 1990. He comments, *'I felt as though I had a bad case of flu, or jet lag a lot of the time. The exhaustion made me clumsy — I'd often spill my food or drinks. I felt like I was unconnected to my body, empty, like a squeezed out tube of toothpaste. I experienced feelings of unprovoked hostility towards my colleagues, especially if they were making new demands on me. Worst of all, despite having entered medicine out of compassion and a desire to help sick people, I found myself resenting the patients. I began dreading each day. Over the months I got more and more ground down, getting increasingly desperate and wondering at times if it might be better to be dead.'*

A junior hospital doctor dies in 1994

Junior hospital doctor dro

Judy Jones
Health Correspondent

A YOUNG doctor collapsed and died after working a gruelling 86-hour week in an NHS hospital.

Officially, the death of Dr Alan Massie, 27, remains a mystery, despite a battery of pathologist's tests to establish the cause. But his distraught parents are convinced that it was due to sheer exhaustion brought on by 'ludicrously long' hours. They are considering suing his employers.

Dr Massie was a popular and highly respected senior house of-

Alan Massie: Exhausted.

ficer at Warrington District General Hospital, Cheshire. He died on 31 January, after working seven of the previous eight days, and three nights. This spell included two unbroken periods of 27 hours and one of 24 hours.

Dr Massie was having to make up for nights missed while on study leave and had spent six months in obstetrics and gynaecology, one of the most demanding medical specialties.

Thousands of junior hospital doctors continue to work dangerously long shifts — 70 to 80-plus hours a week — despite govern-

ment attempts to bring them line with the European Union erage of 59.

The Government's 'New I programme to reduce jun hours established a ceiling c hours a week last April, but 1 doctors still have to work a that level, according to a B Medical Association survey.

According to his pare George and Margaret Massie Massie had frequently been and shattered' in the last months of his life.

On the evening of his deat and his girlfriend, Sharon

The writing on the wall in 1990

A typical, 29-hour, day-in-the-life of Dr Christopher Johnstone. We reproduce in full the entries for this period from Chris Johnstone' diary. During this period he had continuous ECG (brain activity) monitoring. The story told is horrifying. And it is being repeated in hospitals throughout Britain.

25th April

08 20	Start — handover from staff on previous 24 hours. Labour ward round, put in drip.
10 00	Coffee
10 10	To theatre to assist in caesarean section. Bleeped three times in theatre.
11 10	Finish. Sit down.
11 20	To wards.
12 40	Quick lunch.
13 00	Go to lunchtime meeting.
13 30	Called to labour ward. To wards to see patients.
15 00	Talking with woman about serious risk of deformity when her baby is born.
15 10	Called to emergency section (to assist) a difficult one — much bleeding
16 10	Finish, and almost immediately bleeped
16 20	Sick down and get a snack to eat
16 33	Called to labour ward — new patient, see patients on ward.
17 20	Another new patient. Then to labour ward.
18 40	Going round wards.
19 20	Supper (bleeped twice).
20 10	Sit down.
20 12	Bleeped — patient bleeding on ward.
20 36	Another new patient. Then to labour ward.
22 00	Lots happening on labour ward. Very busy!

26th April

00 20	Sit down. Phew!
00 24	Back to work.
00 27	Put in drip. Watch ultrasound.

28

The Observer 10 April 1994

dead after 86-hour week

ere watching television r in a hospital medical ommon room. She said: was really happy and for the first time in ages. just got up to make some was handing me my cup e suddenly said, "I don't ry well . . ." and started

fassie collapsed. Another rushed into the room and suscitation, but failed to im. His father said:- 'I ask Alan, "Why do you work these ludicrously ours?" and he'd reply he

needed to make sure he got good references.

'To see him go downhill over the past six months was terrible. We believe it was the system that killed him. When he was working his body was running on adrenalin — when he had his first chance to relax properly, there was nothing there to keep him going. The day before he died he looked absolutely clapped out.'

Mrs Massie added: 'He had never been ill in his life. All that was wrong with Alan was the hours he had to work.'

The couple are consulting so-

licitors but are unable to act until the cause of death is established and a death certificate issued.

Last Thursday, the Massies heard from Warrington's Coroner's Office that tests on the heart had found nothing abnormal, but that more had been arranged.

Hospital managers say Dr Massie's hours had come down to an average of 72 hours a week in the previous six months. A spokesman said: 'We totally understand and sympathise with the distress of Dr Massie's family. A lot of the staff are still trying to come to terms with what hap-

pened. It is a very sad situation, but it is in the interests of everyone to avoid speculation until the pathologist completes his investigation and submits his findings.'

Mark Porter, a member of the BMA council and of the junior doctors' committee executive, said: 'Obstetrics is a notoriously high-pressure specialty. Although we don't yet know exactly why Dr Massie died, it is recognised that lack of sleep and feeling a tremendous sense of responsibility can occasionally lead to unexplained sudden death.' **Leader, page 26**

01 00	Re-assess woman in premature labour.
01 30	Back to labour ward.
01 42	Sit down.
01 50	Help colleague with episiotomy repair (difficult one).
02 30	Review patients with problems on ward — one in premature labour, one with hypertension.
03 01	Bed.
03 23	Bleeped — tear to suture.
03 30	Get to labour ward — need to have a coffee to wake myself up.
03 45	Explore wound — a difficult tear extending down to anus but not into rectum.
04 00	Call my registrar for advice over phone.
04 10	Start suturing — difficult. I feel tired and know that this woman's future comfort and even sex life is dependent on my doing the job properly. I try hard. EEG shows bursts of theta waves WHILE I AM DOING THIS SUTURING [i.e. Chris was falling asleep through exhaustion] — even though as far as I am aware I was concentrating on the job, and although tired, I'd been much worse on other occasions!
04 50	Finish. Called to see trace. Write notes.
05 24	Get to bed.
07 01	Called — new patient with vaginal bleeding.
08 00	Long discussion with patient who is highly likely to miscarry — explain risks and talk through. I had hoped to do this last night, but was too busy.
08 30	Breakfast.
09 10	Back to wards. Handover. Go round patients and writing notes.
13 00	Finish.

‘If the Authority in this case knew or ought to have known that by requiring him to work the hours they did, they exposed him to risk of injury to his health, then they should not have required him to work in excess of those hours that he safely could have done.’

Lord Justice Stuart Smith
In his judgement [of Dr Christopher Johnstone's case] in the Court of Appeal, December 1990.

Things came to a head when Chris fell asleep at the wheel of his car and drove into a tree when on holiday following a 110-hour working week. Fortunately, no-one was injured but he decided to resign his job and start an action against his employers. He has still not received a penny in compensation and there is no telling when the case might be settled. But he is fighting on behalf of thousands of others in the health service whose health is being sacrificed to the intransigence of managers obsessed with cost cutting and efficiency. His view on the death of Alan Massie: '*I feel very sad that this unnecessary death has happened. The Government and Health Service Management know that these conditions are really dangerous. There's such resistance to change. Even their own (inadequate) recommendations on reducing maximum hours to 72 per week by 1995 are unlikely to be met. I suppose it will only be when human considerations are turned into financial constraints in the form of compensation payouts, that they will actually tackle the problem of excessive hours in the health service. In the meantime, we can only hope that no-one else loses their life.*'

Disorders of the digestive tract

When individuals are under stress, the stomach increases production of hydrochloric acid, which can cause inflammation and eventually lead to sores, or ulcers on the lining of the digestive tract. It has also been suggested that over a long period of time, intense stress levels can increase the risk of developing conditions such as inflammatory bowel disease. In a detailed study of bus work and health, nearly a third of those required to operate an OPO (one person operation) system suffered from some disorder of the digestive system including stomach pain, diarrhoea, constipation, loss of appetite and haemorrhoids (Joffe et al 1986).

Effect on the hormone system

The endocrine system produces chemical messengers or hormones which have an effect on almost every organ in the body. Stress can cause both *over* production and *under* production of several major components of the endocrine system, which in turn affects the major organs including the heart, lungs and brain, as well as the immune system, which is responsible for the body's defence against disease (Cox 1993). Hormones can also affect sleep patterns and induce changes in behaviour.

Damaged defences

The immune system provides the body's defence against disease. Studies show that workers under stress suffer more minor illnesses such as colds and coughs, and may also be at greater risk of developing cancer. It appears that stress can alter the effectiveness of the immune system, and in some circumstances reduce its ability to defend against external infective agents (such as cold viruses) and tumour growth (Cox 1993). Stress can also make worse existing conditions such as asthma, dermatitis and rheumatoid arthritis.

Other physiological effects

In 1990, a major study on the effects of office work on the health of more than 2,000 women working for the Inland Revenue was carried out by researchers from the University of Manchester Institute of Science and Technology (Bramwell and Davidson 1990). The researchers found that there was a clear link between stress at work and menstrual disorders. Few previous studies have considered occupational causes of menstrual disorders — and the medical profession tends to treat only the *symptoms* of menstrual disorders when they are reported. In the London Hazards Centre's previous work with women from a wide range of occupations, menstrual disorders appeared often to be a sensitive indicator of exposure to chemicals, dust, and excessive levels of stress. This anecdotal finding is given more weight by the results of the Inland Revenue study.

In addition to the effects on the menstrual cycle, it has been suggested that stress can affect pregnancy. In particular, work organisation involving shiftwork or nightwork (which is more stressful than fixed day schedules) increases the risk of miscarriage (Infante-Rivard et al 1993) (see page 39). Stress has been implicated as a factor in some of the clusters of miscarriages reported in groups of VDU workers, and work-related fatigue has been shown to increase the risk of premature birth (Colie 1993). Other studies have shown that women in jobs with high demands and low control were more likely to suffer miscarriages, stillbirths, and have low birth-weight babies.

MENTAL HEALTH

Numerous studies of workers in stressful occupations show high levels of mental ill-health. A recent study of stress in UK teachers showed that they are now experiencing stress levels as high as air traffic controllers and GPs (Travers and Cooper 1993). Symptoms of mental ill-health such as anxiety, and depression were common, with poor management structures, constant changes in government policy on schools, and workload being important causes. A similar pattern of stress-related mental ill-health was found by a recent survey of further education lecturers (*NATFHE Journal* Spring 1994). The problems of overload accounted for many of effects on lecturers' health. The following are a few of the quotes extracted from the survey: '*Stress undermines overall confidence so you feel less confident in class with the students*'. '*I have never worked so hard, been so tired, so bad tempered*'. '*The health of our staff is appalling. Most suffer from some form of stress-related illness. Many are teaching while taking anti-depressants or sedatives…it is usual for two or three staff to break down a year*'.

The mental health of blue-collar workers is also at risk from job stress. A three-year study of electrical factory workers in Japan showed that job overload and lack of control over the workplace caused high levels of long-lasting depressive symptoms in the workforce (Kawakami et al 1992). This finding is typical of such studies.

Stress is certainly the primary cause of the condition which has come to be known as 'burn-out'. The three main components of burn-out are emotional exhaustion manifesting as tiredness, irritability, accident proneness, depression and excessive alcohol consumption; 'depersonalisation' — treating other people as if they are objects; and reduced productiveness accompanied by feelings of low achievement. Burn out can occur when mechanisms adopted by individuals for coping with unrelenting stress eventually impair that person's normal functioning.

Tim Nuttall

In the most stressful occupations, in particular in health-care work, levels of suicide are alarmingly high. UK doctors have a 72 per cent greater risk of suicide than the general population (British Medical Association 1992). Of great concern are the statistics showing that doctors practising in the UK but born overseas are at further increased risk of suicide, suggesting that among other factors, discrimination may be adding to already intolerable stress levels.

Post-traumatic stress disorder (PTSD)

Emergency service workers such as firefighters and ambulance staff frequently have to deal with grisly, terrifying and sometimes violent scenes. Following a major disaster some workers may experience extreme anxiety which is often characterised by repeated re-experiencing of the traumatic event. As many as 15 per cent of all front-line London Ambulance staff suffer from PTSD (COHSE 1993). The impact of long-lasting PTSD is considerable and can affect the sufferer's work, family and general quality of life. As more employees such as social workers, bank workers, and housing workers, are exposed to traumatic, violent situations, so more run the risk of developing PTSD.

Several unions whose members are at risk from PTSD have produced guidance and model policies. Details of the policy on responding to incidents of PTSD, negotiated between the train drivers' union ASLEF and British Railways Board, are summarised on page 68 in Part 3 of this book.

PSYCHOSOCIAL EFFECTS

Some of the *ways* in which people try to cope with stress can cause ill-health. Stress is often expressed by the increased consumption of caffeine, alcohol, cigarettes and other drugs such as tranquillisers. In the 1990 survey of women in the Inland Revenue it was found that the higher stress levels among VDU workers compared to non-VDU workers was resulting in increased consumption of alcohol and cigarettes (Bramwell and Davidson 1990). GPs often respond to complaints of stress by prescribing tranquillisers and sleeping pills. Fortunately, the dangerous effects of long-term use of such drugs is now being recognised, as is their inability to tackle the causes of the problem. Smoking causes cancer. Alcohol damages the liver and affects behaviour. Drugs and alcohol can impair the ability to work and disrupt personal relationships which may in turn worsen stress levels.

People under stress can be irritable, withdrawn, appear irrational, aggressive or even violent. This altered behaviour can also impact on relationships inside and outside work. Workers in high-stress occupations are more likely to suffer breakdown of relationships, family break-up and divorce.

Workers under stress are far more likely to have accidents than workers in low stress jobs, and are much more likely to have to take time off work for stress-related sickness. In jobs where work overload is the cause of the stress, the workers find that they have to take time off to deal with the stress, only to return to work to find that the already unmanageable workload has substantially increased in their absence, thereby increasing the source of the stress and fuelling a vicious cycle which may ultimately lead to a complete breakdown in health.

CAUSES OF STRESS (STRESSORS)

Much has been written about the stress rating (known as the Homes-Rahe life stress inventory) assigned to certain life events, ranging from the death of a child or partner which produces the highest stress levels, to changes in social activities which rate lowest on the scale. Whilst acknowledging the impact of factors outside work on overall stress levels, it is the intention of this section to focus principally on *occupational* causes.

The following work factors are all known to contribute to stress:

Physical conditions
▲ noise
▲ poor lighting
▲ overcrowding
▲ extremes of temperature
▲ toxic fumes and chemicals
▲ badly designed furniture
▲ poor maintenance
▲ dangerous equipment
▲ working with VDUs

Balancing the demands of home and work
▲ poor childcare facilities
▲ long hours
▲ need to take time off to care for sick children and other dependants

Job design
▲ work overload
▲ machine-paced work

▲ surveillance and monitoring by computers, videos and listening devices
▲ repetitive work
▲ time pressures
▲ responsibility for lives
▲ uncertain responsibilities
▲ excessive requirements
▲ introduction of new technology
▲ underuse of skills

Relationships in organisation

▲ unsympathetic management
▲ lack of support, assistance or training
▲ harassment (sexism, racism, homophobia, ageism)
▲ customer/client complaints
▲ poor communication
▲ social isolation at work

Work organisation and conditions

▲ low pay
▲ lone working
▲ lack of job security
▲ shiftwork
▲ nightwork
▲ lack of control over work
▲ continuous changes in work organisation
▲ lack of participation in decision-making
▲ financial constraints
▲ rigid hierarchy
▲ harsh disciplinary procedures
▲ inadequate staffing
▲ overpromotion
▲ underpromotion

'Psychosocial factors' is the academic term used to describe all the non-physical characteristics of work structures and organisation that can affect physical as well as mental health, directly or indirectly through the experience of stress.

In the next section we look at some aspects of work organisation that are most likely to contribute to stress.

EXCESSIVE WORKING HOURS

Sudden death is the most extreme consequence of working excessive hours. Physical and psychological fatigue is common. There is an increased risk of heart disease, and victims suffer from sleep difficulties, sexual disorders, gastric disturbances, headaches, backaches, dizziness and weight loss. Accidents become more frequent. There is a range of psychological and behavioural problems: apathy, depression, disorganisation, feelings of incapability, irritability, intolerance, boredom and cynicism. Burn-out, defined as exhaustion, underachievement and the inability to handle personal relationships, can result. In the later stages signs of mental illness can appear. All these effects have knock-on consequences for family and social life (Alfredson et al 1993; Karaki 1991).

Body clocking

The human body works according to circadian rhythms, i.e. body temperature, hormone levels and a variety of other bodily functions vary in an approximately 24-hour cycle. Human performance varies at different times and is lowest at night-time. There is also a dip in early afternoon. There is a biological clock which regulates the cycle and which can function to some degree independently of environmental stimuli. The most important environmental stimulus which does have an effect is the light/dark cycle. This basically enables human beings to function according to the changing times of days and seasons. Knowledge of the time of day and the daily experience of family and social life also help to synchronise the biological and environmental cycles. It has been shown for nightworkers that there is only partial adjustment of the circadian rhythms (Zenz 1988).

NIGHTWORK

There are established health effects of nightwork including fatigue and sleep loss, appetite disturbance, gastrointestinal complaints, heart disease and mood, personality and neurological disorders. There is evidence of menstrual effects and adverse pregnancy outcome in women. There is an increased risk of accidents. There is increased stress on all variations of personal and social life, including relationship breakdown and increased alcohol and drug dependency. Despite all these established health effects, a quarter of British employees work nights, either permanently or as part of a rotating shift pattern (*The Safety and Health Practitioner* 1992).

Sleep difficulties are a major problem for nightworkers, affecting both the duration and quality of sleep. Day sleep after nightwork is generally of shorter duration than normal night sleep and more prone to interruption. It has also been shown to be of poorer quality. After a period of nightwork/day sleep, a sleep deficit can accumulate leading to fatigue. There is some evidence this effect of nightwork is more severe in older workers (*AAOHN Journal* 1991).

About half of nightworkers complain of loss of appetite, resulting both from the non-availability of suitable of suitable food and the requirement to eat at unusual times. This can lead to indigestion and ulcers. Typically the incidence of ulcers increases after about five years' exposure to variable work schedules. A recent study estimated that between 30 and 50 per cent of shiftworkers suffer from gastrointestinal disturbances, a proportion some 5-10 times higher than in day workers (*Health and Safety Information Bulletin* April 1994).

Though it is a matter of dispute, evidence is now accumulating that nightwork does lead to an increase in heart disease (Rosa and Colligan 1992). Groups as diverse as agricultural workers and airline pilots have shown an increased propensity to coronary artery disease and heart attacks after five to ten years on nights. Nightwork has been correlated with increased cholesterol levels, a finding also borne out by animal studies.

Accident rates, both at work and when travelling to and from work, are affected by sleepiness and napping. The particular danger period is late on in shifts shortly after a transition from day to nightwork. This is when the body has had the least opportunity to adjust its ordinary rhythm. This effect has been demonstrated over a wide range of occupations (Gold et al 1992).

It has been pointed out that many disasters occur on the night shift; Three Mile Island, Chernobyl, Bhopal and Exxon Valdez are quoted as examples.

A study of the work schedules of women suffering spontaneous abortions or fetal death showed that women working evening or night shifts were three to four time more likely to suffer pregnancy loss than women working day shifts (Infante-Rivard et al 1993). The authors allowed for all other factors and concluded that pregnancy loss should be considered an additional hazard of evening and nightwork. The European Union Directive on pregnant workers will generate new rights on nightwork. Pregnant women and new mothers who obtain a medical certificate stating that it is necessary for their safety or health will have the right to transfer to suitable day work or go on paid leave. At the time of writing, it remains to be seen how the Health and Safety Commission will translate the Directive into UK Regulations, but the proposals put out for consultation leave something to be desired.

The new European legislation follows in part the recommendations of the International Labour Office which adopted a detailed set of proposals at a conference in 1990 (see Part 3).

SHIFTWORK

All the health effects of nightwork are compounded by rotating shift arrangements. On permanent nights, the biological clock can adapt to a degree, but with variable shifts this is less possible. Thus, all the stresses resulting from disruption of the circadian rhythms are increased by the constant alteration of working hours.

The Health and Safety Executive has produced two major reviews of the health effects of shiftwork (Harrington 1978; Waterhouse 1990). Harrington in particular was highly critical of many reports of adverse health effects of shiftwork, dismissing many of them on methodological grounds. He denied that there was a link between shiftwork and heart disease or neurological problems. He was of the opinion that repetitive tasks associated with low motivation and fatigue were performed less well at night but that interesting jobs were less affected. He also rejected any clear relationship between the time of day and the frequency of accidents. The later report does modify the position on cardiovascular illness and neurological problems but still takes an ambivalent attitude to the link between accidents and shiftwork. Much discussion goes into the differences among individuals in the effect of shiftwork and there is a list of the medical factors that should be taken into account in counselling workers against shiftwork:

▲ those with gastric or duodenal ulcers

▲ those with recurrent problems of indigestion and related disorders

▲ those on chronic medication in which the timing is important — insulin-dependent diabetics and those with severe thyroid or adrenal pathologies would fall into this category

▲ those with severe neurological problems, particularly depressives who might be adversely by altered light/dark schedules

▲ those with chronic heart disorders

▲ those with chronic sleep disorders

▲ epileptics, as treatment is hampered by irregular sleep-wake schedules and sleep deficit can increase the tendency to seizures

A number of other factors are also explored including age, physiology, personality and social effects. One of Harrington's observations has been widely quoted elsewhere. This is that 10 per cent of shiftworkers enjoy shiftwork, most put up with it and 20-30 per cent find it unpleasant enough to leave. In a paper which prides itself on its scientific rigour, it is somewhat surprising to find that this assertion is based only on a personal communication and not on published research. The trade union COHSE (now part of UNISON) puts it rather differently: '*10 per cent of shiftworkers enjoy nightwork and this means that 90 per cent have to put up with nightwork unwillingly or are forced to leave due to ill-health*' (COHSE 1992). At any rate it can be surmised that workers put up with shiftwork because the alternatives on offer are low pay and unemployment.

A huge amount of research has focused on the differences among individuals as a means of establishing the best means of adapting to or coping with shiftwork. This places the emphasis on the individual modifying his/her lifestyle to suit the demands of the job. One questionable approach advocates personality 'hardiness' training (Wedderburn 1994). Wedderburn reports that training in commitment to the job and acceptance of change can reconcile workers to shiftwork and reduce the incidence of digestive problems. He also reports that employees often resist educative attempts to change their habits. Well, yes, why shouldn't they?

A comprehensive set of recommendations for adapting the worker to the job can be found in a 1991 report by a Dublin-based research organisation (European Foundation for the Improvement of Living and Working Conditions 1991). This contains advice on handling sleep problems, eating, physical fitness and keeping up social contacts. There are no less than 36 hints on avoiding sleep deprivation. Some of these verge on the comical, e.g. 'Have you thought of rotating your bedroom?' This turns out to mean finding the quietest place to sleep in your home in the daytime. Other advice is to move to a quieter part of town. Evidently, mansions for shiftworkers is the answer.

However well-meaning all of this is, it indicates the upheaval required to mitigate the effects of shiftwork. All the recommendations on diet and exercise are impeccable and add up to a guide to a healthy lifestyle. They also require quite a substantial disposable income. This is equally the case for the suggestions on maintaining social contacts which make important points on the role of trade unions. Shiftworkers are advised to insist on special meetings with trade union officers at times which suit everyone, to have a representative available for workers on all shifts, and to ensure that some shiftworkers become union representatives.

A great deal of research has also been carried out on adapting the job to the worker, i.e. investigating shiftwork patterns to establish those that have the least effect on health. A very wide range of shift patterns has been developed:
▲ treble-shift non-continuous — three consecutive shifts per day providing 24-hour cover, five days per week; rotation of shifts, e.g. changing shift each week with a three-week cycle
▲ alternating days and nights — two shifts per day operating five days per week; workers employed alternately with one week on days, one week on nights
▲ double days — two shifts per day — one in morning, one in afternoon, no nightwork; workers alternate between shifts

▲ permanent nights — night shift for four or five nights per week

▲ evening or twilight shift — part-time shift in late afternoon or evening

▲ mini-shifts — two or three rotating or overlapping shifts of about five hours each, normally operating during the daytime

▲ rotating days — six or seven days cover per week with workers working five days per week

▲ weekend shifts — workers work Saturday and Sunday only, as an addition to double day or treble shiftworking carried out by other workers during the week

▲ split shifts — workers have two or more periods of work per day separated by long break of two hours or more

▲ eight-hour continuous — three eight-hour shifts per day with workers working on each shift with various types of rotation

▲ 12-hour continuous — two 12-hour shifts per day with workers working on each shift with a variety of rotas.

Recommendations on constructing shift patterns that have minimal effect are detailed in Part 3.

There is a consensus on permanent nights; circadian rhythms adjust completely for only a few people and people on permanent nights do become socially isolated (that small proportion of workers who claim to like nightwork are reported to find this the attraction). Sleep deficit builds up with a succession of nights and there is some evidence that the probability of accidents increases after two night shifts. Quickly rotating patterns offer more stability for social contacts than weekly rotated shifts or permanent nights. The earlier a morning shift starts, the more likely is a reduction of sleep time in order to wake, rise and travel. Though shift change times are often regarded as rigid, flexible changeover times can be introduced even for three-shift systems and this can give individuals more scope for sleeping arrangements and social contacts.

The main arguments against short intervals between shifts are the practical ones of not being able to fit in essential non-work activities, especially sleep. Such arrangements sometimes seem attractive as a way of packing in a lot of work time quickly in order to create bigger blocks of time off. They are, however, known to produce high levels of fatigue. The argument about dead time between work periods also applies to split shifts. Compressed working weeks, i.e. long periods of continuous work followed by extended time off, are attractive not so much for leisure activities but for the opportunity to do a second job. Young workers with high financial needs are more likely to be tempted by such arrangements but older workers (i.e. those who survive) attest to their exhausting nature.

There are contradictory reports on the effect of the length of shifts. Rapidly rotating 12-hour shifts have been recommended and there have been suggestions that the incidence of adverse health effects for 12 hours is no greater than for eight-hour shifts. There are plenty of reports of microsleep, napping and human error beginning to rise six hours into shifts, resulting in increased accident rates. Accidents by truck and bus drivers are particularly notable in this respect. Two views are advanced on the relative length of night versus day shifts. On the one hand, it is argued that where the effort involved in the job is roughly the same at all times, the night shift should be relatively shorter in view of the extra strain in maintaining the same level of performance. For example, the night shift could be seven hours and the other two 8.5 hours. On the other hand, where the nightwork is lighter than that during the day, a longer night shift may be a possibility. There are a number of issues which are so far unresolved and this is one area where the health and safety arguments do not indicate the best practice.

It is argued that circadian rhythms adjust better to forward rotating shifts than to backward ones. Workers on forward rotating schedules report greater alertness and less fatigue than those on backwards cycles. It also seems that there is more napping on the job in backwards cycles. There do not appear to be reports supporting the contrary point of view. In distinction to the view above, some opinion favours slowly rather than rapidly rotating shifts, the former providing more time to adjust to the change in arrangements. This is another area where research is incomplete and where workers should ensure that their own needs and experience are paramount.

A number of unions (COHSE, GMB) have advised their members of the effects of shift and nightwork and the TUC has now taken it up as a campaign issue. A number of motions were carried at the 1993 Congress on the relationship between working hours and stress and instructing the General Council to identify and publicise best practice in the prevention and alleviation of work-related stress. However, it has to be confessed that trade union practice does not always measure up to the demands of the situation. A GMB member wrote in to his union journal to complain that shiftwork was ruining plans to start a family (*GMB Journal* May 1994). He and his wife had been put on separate shifts and had now started quarrelling whenever they managed to spend time together. Moreover his sex drive seemed to have gone. However, the advice he got in return was less than adequate — '*Many couples working shifts will know exactly how helpless you are feeling. Pressures of work can often play havoc with our privates lives. But the important thing to remember is that no-one is to blame and there are solutions to your problem.*' The solutions, apart from the partners getting together on the same shift, purely consisted in adjustments to their personal life, including putting their family plans on hold. The poor member was assured that 'these simple measures' really would work. No suggestion here that you could blame the bosses, question whether the shiftwork was really necessary in the first place or take collective industrial or political action to improve things. Yet it might be suggested that it is only in these ways that real changes can be effected.

VIOLENCE AS A SOURCE OF STRESS

A recent survey of union representatives covering 90,000 workers in local government, the civil service, passenger transport services, postal services, education, the health service, the probation service, the retail industry and banking and finance found that over 70 per cent of the workplaces had experienced violent incidents in the last two years (*Bargaining Report* May 1994). These incidents included verbal abuse, threats and actual physical assault.

Workers who routinely experience violence at work, the threat of violence or anxiety about violence can expect their lives to be dominated by stress and its effects. Violence arises from either,

a) the context of the work, for example:
▲ transport workers being assaulted by drunks and muggers

▲ education workers being verbally and physically attacked
▲ care workers being assaulted and injured by those in their care
▲ people working with money being robbed
▲ travelling service workers being attacked on visits

Or,

b) the system of work, for example:
▲ verbal abuse from line managers who lack supervisory skills
▲ 'rat-packing' (the situation where, when one person begins to pick on another, others join in so that all are now picking on the victim) and other forms of scapegoating by peers
▲ sexual and racial harassment or abuse
▲ open and implied management threats, used as 'stimulators'
▲ unnecessary application of workplace disciplinary codes

> At Essex University, a joint staff union, management and student union group has set up a team of Harassment Advisers as part of their equal opportunities programme. As well as dealing with sexual and racial harassment, advisers have been asked to deal with incidents of bullying. Although no formal evaluation of the project has yet taken place, the initial stages have produced encouraging results.

Many employers are loath to tackle violence at work and will go to extreme lengths to avoid reducing it. A bus drivers' branch of the Transport and General Workers Union was de-recognised by their company because they put management under pressure to install safety screens partially to protect drivers from attack from behind. Yet, other bus companies have applied to Traffic Commissioners to withdraw services from routes dangerous to their drivers.

Employers often use forms of violence as a 'management' control technique. Abusive line managers who threaten and frighten workers are not seen as 'attackers' but can be rewarded by productivity payments for their bullying behaviour. They are not disciplined for their despicable actions.

The HSE defines violence as,

'any incident in which an employee is abused, threatened or assaulted by a member of the public in circumstances arising from her or his employment.'

This is a restrictive definition that reflects the HSE's apparent concession to employer's lobbies. It is clear that there is a contradiction in the HSE's position on violence: violent behaviour towards an employee by a 'member of the public' *is violence* but exactly the same behaviour by a working colleague or manager is not.

The important point in terms of tackling and eliminating violence at work is to ignore the artificial category being promoted by the HSE and to treat *all* violence as the hazard to health that it indisputably is. In Part 3 we set out some of the elements which should be incorporated in any policy on tackling violence at work.

PHYSICAL CONDITIONS

A working environment designed without consideration of individual worker's needs, which is uncomfortable, unsafe or unhealthy, can cause stress or add to stress caused by psychosocial factors. Equipment manufactured for use in work frequently takes no account of the physical characteristics of those who will operate it. It may be introduced into the workplace without considering its effect on temperature, noise, ventilation and overcrowding.

Noise

High levels of noise directly damage the middle and inner ears causing impairment of hearing. Lower levels can interfere with communication and, particularly if prolonged, cause anxiety, irritability and tension, increase fatigue and affect efficiency (Cox 1993). A 1992 study of more than 2,000 blue-collar workers over a two-year period found that exposure to noise, even *below* levels considered harmful to *hearing*, caused high levels of distress, anxiety, accidents and sick leave (Melamed et al 1992). As well as causing symptoms of mental ill-health, workers exposed for long periods of time to high noise levels have a high incidence of allergies, respiratory and digestive disorders and musculo-skeletal and heart problems (Cox 1993).

Noise levels as high as 98 decibels — capable of causing hearing damage and stress — have been measured in Oxford Street stores as music is blasted out to attract customers from the street.
London Hazards Centre

WHO SUFFERS MOST?

In its 1992 publication on preventing stress at work, the International Labour Office (ILO) reported evidence that workers in a wide and growing range of occupations are at risk from stress. The following is a list of occupations with high stress levels which have been the subject of research studies. As conditions of work deteriorate throughout the cost-cutting 1990s, many other occupations may be added to this list.

Air-traffic controllers
Blue-collar workers
Bus and truck drivers
Civil servants

Construction workers
Firefighters
Healthcare professionals
Journalists
Miners
Police
Postal workers
Social workers
Teachers

More shop floor than top floor

Contrary to popular opinion, recent research shows that stress-related illness is lowest among professional and managerial groups and highest among blue-collar workers (*Independent on Sunday* 28 November 1993). Early results from a large-scale, community-wide survey being carried out by Professor Cooper showed high levels of stress amongst people with low levels of job satisfaction, often those employed on repetitive menial tasks.

Women

Recent studies have shown that women workers are at greater risk of stress-related illness than men doing the same job. This is not (as is sometimes claimed) because of some physiological weakness peculiar to women, but because they have, on average, significantly less control at work. Women are over-represented in areas of employment in which they have little control, such as the retail, office work, garment, catering, healthcare and outworking (homeworking) industries. Sexual harassment, reported by 70 per cent of women surveyed in London, adds significantly to stress at work.

Taking into account women's paid work in the workplace, and unpaid work at home, a woman with two or three children works 80-90 hours per week. Managing two jobs can make life difficult and stressful, for example trying to fit shopping into a lunch break or needing time off work when children are sick. Family responsibilities often dictate how far they can travel for work, and for some this means working in the home, where they remain isolated, and easily exploited. Women are more vulnerable in times of economic recession where their jobs (especially part-time jobs) are the first to go. There is little provision of services that might help to alleviate some of the stress, such as affordable childcare facilities and improved public transport.

In the previous sections we have looked at the symptoms, effects and causes of stress on workers' health and wellbeing. In Part 3 we look at strategies for the prevention of stress, employers' duties, the law and the trade union response.

3

STRATEGIES FOR TACKLING STRESS AT WORK

STRESS IS A TRADE UNION ISSUE

Tackling stress is a complex problem for trade unionists and workers, since the causes of stress are such fundamentals as lack of workers' control over the working arrangements, insufficient staffing levels, and the need to work long hours to earn a decent wage. Clearly such issues are challenging, but any trade union strategy must focus on removing the causes of stress at source, rather than trying simply to deal with the symptoms and teach people how to cope with unacceptable levels of occupational stress.

The mythology surrounding stress has trivialised the mental and physical anguish suffered by all sorts of workers made ill by their jobs. It is an attempt to divide the world into copers and non-copers. Of course, this victim-blaming approach is nothing new in relation to any workplace hazard. The myth of the careless worker is pernicious.. Treating stress as an individual problem to be solved in an individual way is an approach that is always destined to fail. Very often lifestyle factors are highlighted — exercise, diet and so on. However, workers who have no choice or control over their working environment or the organisation of their work, workers who do dirty, dangerous, monotonous low-paid work are scarcely going to be impressed by the benefits of the typical ready-made stress solutions, such as taking up yoga or joining a squash club.

> Anne Greaves of the UNISON Health and Safety Unit, (formerly Health and Safety Officer for NALGO) was one of the first union health and safety officials to produce accessible guidance for safety representatives on tackling stress in the workplace. Speaking to

the London Hazards Centre about the hundreds of representatives that have used *Tackling Occupational Stress* over the years she said: *'This document was important because it focused on stress as a collective, rather than an individual, issue. Representatives reported that raising the issue in this way reduced the alienation of individual members and changed the agenda for joint union management meetings from considering only counselling, to considering a stress prevention policy for everyone'.*

Stress is not a mysterious ailment suffered by individuals who are either unfortunate or incompetent. As we have shown, stress is suffered as a direct result of a poor working environment, poor job design, poor contractual arrangements and poor management of work organisation. Trade unions can negotiate to reduce stress in the same way as any other occupational hazard.

Difficult as it may be, tackling occupational stress provides trade unions with the ideal and legitimate opportunity systematically to investigate job design and work organisation as well as integrating this with the more traditional workplace environment inspections which trade union safety representatives carry out.

The aims in tackling occupational stress must include:
▲ employer recognition of the legal responsibility to prevent occupational stress (see page 84)
▲ employer recognition that workers are experiencing occupational stress
▲ the establishment of a negotiated management/union policy on occupational stress that is implemented in practice, monitored for its effectiveness, and regularly reviewed with the aim of progressive improvement. The safety committee should be used to set this up, with the involvement of the shop stewards committee where one exists.
▲ recognition that there are no magic solutions to banish stress from the workplace. There has to be an ongoing process, which involves every level of the workforce and has commitment from the highest levels of management.
▲ the policy must be in the clear context of a preventive strategy,

encompassing the principle in health and safety law that work should be adapted to the worker, not the other way round (see page 86)

▲ reporting systems must be set up to allow early recognition of symptoms and detection of causes

▲ workers suffering from stress should be assisted and protected from loss of pay or status

▲ management must agree actively to involve workers and unions in planning work organisation

▲ ultimately, management must be willing to relinquish and devolve some of its control over work organisation.

COUNTERING ARGUMENTS AGAINST RECOGNITION OF OCCUPATIONAL STRESS

Clearly it is easier for management to point to factors outside work which contribute to stress. (Even in cases of exposure to toxic substances at work employers and their lawyers will argue that the victim's illness was caused by smoking, for example.)

This tendency to concentrate on non-workplace stressors is encouraged by much of the popular literature on stress, which considers the psychological and emotional impact of long lists of life events, such as death of close relative, death of spouse, moving house and so on. Usually only a few items correspond to people's working lives, such as redundancy or having a serious illness/accident (although work-related accidents and illnesses are rarely explicitly mentioned).

So, the first thing to get clear is that it is understood that there are many factors outside work which also contribute to stress, not least transport to and from work! However, we are not looking at the kind of 'How stressed are you?' lifestyle questionnaires published in popular magazines. The information on the causes and symptoms of occupational stress given in Part 2, can be used to establish an agreed list of workplace factors which may give rise to stress, and those symptoms which are agreed to be associated with them.

There are three main problem areas we may anticipate that employers will throw up.

1. Managers will not accept that their employees are genuinely experiencing symptoms of stress and that this is caused by work.

2. If managers do accept that workers are experiencing occupational stress, they will not treat it as a collective or organisational problem, but will only treat it as a problem affecting some susceptible individuals.

3. Managers may refuse to act at all, or to respond appropriately.

> Up until recently, London Ambulance Service accident and emergency staff suffering from severe stress reactions of Post Traumatic Stress Disorder were referred to outside agencies such as MIND or Relate, and were charged up to £50 a session from their wages (GMB 1993).

MANAGEMENT STRESS PREVENTION STRATEGIES

In contrast with the CBI's claim that 60 per cent of UK companies design jobs to alleviate stress (see page 23), the Health and Safety Executive reports that *'only a minority of organisations appear to be directly and deliberately addressing the management of occupational stress'* (Cox 1993). Of those companies which do, only a few concentrate on stress *prevention*. Some companies have strategies for reacting when problems arise, and others offer rehabilitation to help workers recover only after the event.

Within each of these categories, there is often a further distinction between companies operating policies which focus on the *organisation* and those that focus on *individual* stress management.

An individual approach

Despite a lack of evidence supporting the effectiveness of such programmes, a large proportion of stress management activity in the UK and US is individually focused, designed for managerial and white-collar workers and concerned with changing the worker rather than the work or work environment. This has a great deal to do with the nature and influence of management views in this country. According to the HSE's report, in Scandinavia, where responsibility for working conditions is shared more equally between labour and management groups, organisational approaches to stress management are more common (Cox 1993). In the US, the dominance of management views has been largely responsible for the development of Employee Assistance Programmes (EAPs).

Employee Assistance Programmes

EAPs largely consist of counselling and helplines for individual employees and focus on issues such as drug abuse, personal difficulties and family problems. The assumption used is that it is the failure of the worker to deal with these issues that is the root cause of stress. More sinisterly, it has been suggested that EAPs could be used by employers to demonstrate that they have 'given workers a chance' in order to meet legal requirements to enable the employer to sack the worker. However, it could equally be argued that using EAP provision alone demonstrates that the employer has failed to carry out adequate risk assessments (see page 86) and eliminate the hazards.

Workers at a major glass manufacturer have discovered that, far from considering stress reduction programmes following restructuring, management are more likely to discipline sick workers. One worker disciplined while on long-term sick leave died from cancer before he could attend an appeal against the disciplinary action. Others have lost long-term benefit for being off sick for more than seven days in the past three years.

Stress management training

Another popular method of palming off responsibility for stress management on to individual employees is stress management training. This consists largely of training in such techniques as meditation and relaxation. Whilst we are not suggesting that these techniques in themselves are harmful, they are not designed to reduce or eliminate sources of stress at work, but only to teach workers more effective coping strategies. The reliance on such techniques may in the end contribute to ill-health as follows: by failing to tackle the causes of stress, the symptoms of stress inevitably recur. The worker feels frustrated and disappointed that the stress management training has failed and is conscious of failing the employer's expectations and this in turn exacerbates the stress.

We need to develop approaches to get management to adopt a more enlightened and positive attitude.

Tim Nuttall

TACKLING STRESS IN YOUR WORKPLACE

1. Raising the issue
Firstly, management must be convinced that there is a genuine and work-related problem. This attitude is gradually becoming easier to overcome as there is increasingly widespread recognition that stress has undesirable

consequences for workers' health and, furthermore, presents costly economic hazards for businesses (see page 22). Stress is a hot health and safety topic internationally and in the UK; it is a 'priority area' for the European Commission. The Trades Union Congress (TUC) designated stress a priority area for action, and has set up a team to develop guidelines on a practical approach to the identification, assessment and control of stress (TUC 1993), Most trade unions have now produced guidance on the subject.

The problem remains, how do you convince your employer that stress is a problem in your particular workplace? In the same way as you convince your employer that any other occupational hazard exists and has to be acted upon! First you need the kind of information set out in Part 2. This general information, and any sector/industry-specific information you can find, then has to be applied to your workplace.

Trade union safety representatives have the legal right, under the Safety Representatives and Safety Committees (SRSC) Regulations 1978, *'to investigate potential hazards at the workplace'*. So representatives can inspect for risk factors, and talk to workers about what they perceive to be workplace stressors. The point is to raise the issue at work at all levels. Talk to union members, organise meetings, get information from the union and other sources, give information to workers and start getting ideas from them about what the big problems are as they see them and what they think might be done to alleviate them. You may find it very useful to carry out a union survey to see what symptoms members are suffering and what they think the causes are (see page 91). Start to develop some ideas for priority action, and proposals to put to management.

Raise the issue with management — you can point out any indications that stress exists, give examples of good practice from other companies, give them copies of articles, information from the trade union or the TUC, this book and so on. Use the Safety Committee if you have one; if you do not have one then see if you can set one up (see page 90).

When you draw stress to management's attention you can discuss their legal responsibilities (see page 84) under the Health and Safety at Work (HSW)

Act and particularly under the Management of Health and Safety at Work (MHSW) Regulations which say that employers must carry out a risk assessment to evaluate risk factors in the workplace, find out who may be at risk and to what degree they may be affected by stress at work. If you can argue that there is any degree of risk to workers of occupational stress, or that a problem already exists, then the employer is obliged to carry out a written risk assessment and to control the risk adequately.

2. Don't blame the victim

The second big problem is that, very often, if management accepts that workers are suffering work-related stress, they will not treat this as an organisational, collective problem; instead they will offer stress counselling or stress management courses, any kind of individual solution to help the poor unfortunates who cannot cope. In other words, they want the workers to adapt so that they can cope with an unsatisfactory working environment. Counselling indicates a failure to control work-related stress. Counselling should be used only to help people who have already been affected, but the main emphasis should be on prevention, and counselling should form only a small part of the whole strategy to avoid and control stress.

Individual solutions do not work because they do not make any attempt to solve the problem. The International Labour Office (ILO) criticises *'self appointed experts with pre-packaged programmes good for any occasion and situation, and remedial interventions focused on the effects rather than the causes of stress'* (International Labour Office 1992). Their detailed evaluation of case histories concludes that the least useful approach was person-based interventions such as counselling and relaxation techniques. These were found to be ineffective even where employers had invested considerable time and resources. The goal is to improve the working environment, not just to patch up those casualties of it who remain in the job.

Professor Cox in his 1994 publication commissioned by the HSE says: *'Practice in relation to the management of occupational stress is subject to a number of criticisms. First, too narrow a view has been taken of what constitutes stress management and there has been too strong a focus on 'caring for or curing' the individual.'*

'*Second, much of what has been offered, even in this narrow respect, has either a weak theoretical base, or has been developed from outside occupational stress research.*'

'*Third, there has been a tendency to treat the application of stress management strategies as a self contained action and divorce that application from any preceding process of problem diagnosis.*'

The European Commission Health and Safety Directorate recommends that: '*Interventions directed towards individuals should support them in crisis situations, enabling them to have more control over their lives and access to coping resources. Blaming the victim is not the right approach, so programmes directed towards the individual worker are never a substitute for more comprehensive strategies designed to tackle the problem of stress at source*' (*Hygeia* 1992).

The consensus now, from most quarters, is that a 'problem solving' preventive approach aimed at improving the working environment is what is required, rather than only trying to deal with symptoms experienced by individuals, important as that is as an additional activity.

3. Getting management to act

So, the third and biggest hurdle then, is getting management to act, and to act appropriately.

CONTROLLING STRESS

As with all types of occupational hazard, the most effective way of protecting workers' health is to eliminate or control the hazard, or cause of ill-health. This applies as much to stress, as it does to exposure to poisonous chemicals or dusts.

Ronald Haig, Head of the Industrial Medicine Unit of the European Commission states their view: '*As regards the management of occupational risks, it is becoming increasingly apparent that the subjective notion of well-being at work must be considered in the same light as occupational accidents and illness.*'

This concept of controlling the hazard (rather than changing the worker) is a fundamental requirement of UK health and safety law (see page 86). Controlling stress at source requires a thorough and coherent policy on stress prevention, involving everyone in the workplace. There follow some examples of policies and advice on formulating policy, including recent legislation on the subject of stress management from Sweden. In formulating a policy for your workplace you may wish to extract from these policies the features most appropriate for your workplace and situation.

Two important points to make to management are firstly, that employers have legal obligations to prevent stress (see page 84), and secondly, that a comprehensive stress prevention policy can be expected to yield concrete economic benefits from improved productivity and staff morale, and reduced sickness absence and staff turnover.

The Civil Service Occupational Health Service (CSOHS) has found that 5 million working days, costing £450 million, are lost each year due to sickness absence in the Civil Service (Civil Service Occupational Health Service 1993). In a report to managers, the CSOHS advised that, *'sickness absence is related to some circumstances at work, including monotony and lack of individual control of work, the failure perceived by employees to utilise fully their skills, and repetitive processes.'* The report goes on to recommend that: *'Departments and agencies should review the organisation of their work and the processes and practices entailed in the jobs done by their staff. The broad intention should be to provide greater job satisfaction. To influence sickness absence this should be achieved by making greater use of individual skills, by providing individuals with more responsibility and control over thier work, and by avoiding monotonous and unchanging job activities. Changing the nature of inidividual jobs in this way represents a very considerable challenge to managers at every level in the Civil Service. If they are discussed with staff and implemented in conjunction with staff these measures will undoubtedly reduce sickness absence.* (Our emphasis).

> '*It costs money to reduce sickness absence but the real benefit is the financial saving that will accrue as a result of the reduction. There will be other less definable benefits too — amongst them more effective and efficient performance and improvement in staff morale, in addition to improvements in individual health.*'

Worker participation

An absolutely fundamental criterion for successful action is worker participation. The International Labour Office (ILO) found that initiatives that didn't involve worker participation were unsuccessful (International Labour Office 1992). '*Active involvement of workers in planning or significant worker participation in group discussions on environmental changes were generally strongly associated with success.*'

The ILO report goes on to conclude '*Management's willingness to take the 'risk' to relinquish some of its control over work organisation is undoubtedly an important factor in programme success*'.

They also point out that '*The degree of union participation…is associated clearly with programme success.*'

STRESS PREVENTION POLICIES

The EC sets out the following *principles* for designing a stress prevention strategy at the workplace.

Principles of stress prevention

Just as there are many causes, so there is no unique cure for stress. Several principles are important, however, in designing a stress prevention strategy at the workplace:

Prevention through improved design

Action must start at the design stage. Facilities, equipment, machinery and tools have to be planned having in mind the potential health impact. Company buying policies need to consider their future impact on employees' well-being.

Participation of end users

Technocratic approaches should be avoided. Joint initiatives of managers, workers and professionals are the key to success, and top-down management strategies should be replaced by an involvement approach.

Better work organisation

This means greater control and autonomy by workers over their tasks, less monotonous and repetitive jobs with greater social interaction and workgroup support.

A holistic approach to the environment

Both the physical and the social environments should be integrated, while both the working and living environments should also be considered as one in terms of their effects on occupational stress.

An enabling organisational culture

A healthy company should be measured by the quality of working life for its workforce and not only by economic values. The benefits from such an approach should be gauged in the medium and long term, not in the short term.

Attention to workers with special needs

Such as shift workers, migrant workers, older and young workers. The gender dimension also needs to be taken into account.

Economic feasibility

Economic feasibility of the prevention strategy will provide support for the policies and will increase the chance of success and commitment by the organisation (*Hygeia* 1992).

The International Federation of Commercial, Clerical, Professional, and Technical Employees (FIET) made the following points in 1992 on formulating a policy on occupational stress:

FIET recommendations on limitation of work-related stress and pressure affecting salaried employees

1. Preventive health protection starts with the way work is organised.
2. Trade union representatives must be involved in a comprehensive and timely fashion in deciding how work is organised and carried out.
3. This involvement also includes staffing requirements (personnel planning), as well as the introduction or modification of personnel information and performance evaluation systems.
4. Work schedules which cause great strain (eg night and shift work) are to be eliminated or reduced.
5. Work is to be organised in such a way that the individual worker can have independence and responsibility.
6. Measures to prevent, alleviate or compensate work-related pressures must not be subordinate to purely economic considerations.
7. Initial and further training opportunities must be offered which take the current and future qualification requirements of employees into consideration. This also includes a role for the trade unions in determining the contents of training courses in order to ensure that preventive health protection is included.
8. Individuals' rights to more self and co-determination at and about work must be revised.
9. Legislators are called upon to take into account the increase of stress-related illnesses by further developing social legislation (recognition of stress-related illnesses as occupational illnesses).

10. As an accompaniment to the above-named measures, environmental measures at the workplace must be further developed in collective and company agreements (FIET 1992).

To FIET's recommendations we would add the following points:

1. Monotonous, repetitive and isolated work should be reduced to a minimum.
2. Pay should not be linked to individual productivity.
3. Stress prevention should be included in the planning of workplace design, facilities, equipment and machinery.
4. Employers should take account of the combined effect of home and work pressures and provide facilities which relieve those pressures (such as childcare facilities).

With stress becoming increasingly recognised as a priority health and safety issue for trade unions, as well as producing guidance for members, several UK trade unions have passed conference motions on tackling stress at work. Examples of motions from a civil service union and a teachers' union are given in the boxes below.

'Conference believes that prevention of work-related stress is a priority. We note that the Health and Safety Executive are committed to issuing Guidance to Employers on the issue which whilst welcomed is not enough. Conference instructs the National Executive Committee to:

1. Seek from the Civil Service Occupational Health Service a definitive list of stress-related illnesses.

2. Examine work processes amongst CSPA grades with a view to recommending ways of reducing stress.

3. Publish guidance to employees on how to avoid stress.

4. Seek work-related stress cases from branches with a view to taking legal action against the Government where such cases are considered strong.' (Civil and Public Services Association 1994).

'*Conference congratulates those local authorities which have recognised the detrimental effects of the increasing incidence of stress-related illness amongst teachers, and have attempted to tackle the issue positively.*

However, Conference notes with alarm the increasing levels of occupational stress in teaching and recognises that major contributory factors include:

1. *Workload pressures*
2. *The impact of incessant Government education initiatives*
3. *Dictatorial and unsympathetic management styles*
4. *Lack of consultation and poor internal communications in schools*
5. *Worsening physical conditions of school buildings.*

Conference calls upon all LEAs, governing bodies and school managements to accept their responsibility for the health, safety and welfare of their workforce and demands the adoption of management styles which promote a healthy and stress-free working environment.

Conference pledges full support to sick members and calls upon local and negotiating secretaries and health and safety co-ordinators to continue discussions with the relevant bodies with a view to the creation and adoption of stress at work policy statements which start by addressing the causes of stress in teaching before suggesting measures intended merely to ameliorate the condition.' (NASUWT 1994).

Selected recommendations of APA/NIOSH panel on work design and stress 1992

Control

1. Workers should be given the opportunity to control various aspects of their work and workplace. A way of accomplishing such control is through participative decision-making.

2. Systems should have optimal response times or optimal response ranges.

Uncertainty

1. Employees should have information in as timely and complete a form as possible.
2. Work assignments should be clear and unambiguous.
3. Organisations should make clear policy statements and apply those policies in a consistent manner.
4. Employees should have easy access to information sources.

Conflict

1. Participative decision-making should be used to reduce conflict.
2. Job descriptions and task assignments should be clear and stable.
3. Mechanisms should be introduced for the management of conflict.
4. There should be open discussion of potential and real conflicts in organisational settings.
5. Supervisors should adopt supportive styles to reduce conflict.
6. Demands should not exceed resources.

Task/job demands

1. A variety of knowledge, skills and abilities should be required by a job.
2. Workers should receive feedback about performance.
3. Organisations should not pay people to endure boring work.
4. Service work should not be patterned after the assembly line.
5. Feedback should be provided to service workers.
6. Information-based jobs should be enlarged rather than reduced in scope.

Amendments to Swedish Working Environment Act 1991 (to include psycho-social hazards in work organisation)

1. Working conditions are to be adapted to people's physical and psychological conditions.

2. Employees are to be given opportunities of participating in the arrangement of their own work situation, its transformation and development.

3. Technology, the organisation of work and job contents are to be designed so that the employee is not exposed to physical or mental loads that may lead to ill-health or accidents.

4. Forms of remuneration and work schedules that involve an appreciable risk of ill-health or accidents are not to be used.

5. Strictly controlled or tied work is to be avoided or restricted.

6. Work should afford opportunities for variety, social contacts, co-operation and a connection between individual tasks.

7. Working conditions should provide opportunities for personal and occupational development, as well as for self-determination and professional responsibility.

DEALING WITH INDIVIDUAL WORKERS SUFFERING FROM STRESS

Although it is always preferable to prevent ill-health before it arises, in practice union representatives may be called on to represent individual members who are already victims of stress. As well as considering the workplace causes, which may be affecting other members, union representatives should bear in mind the following priorities:

▲ to protect the member's health and job
▲ to insist on a second medical opinion, where the member's job depends on it
▲ to solve the immediate problem (for example, temporary sick leave, transfer, re-allocation of work)
▲ to ensure the member is getting the right sort of professional health
▲ to investigate the underlying cause of the problem with other union members
▲ to remove, or reduce, the causes of workplace stress (Labour Research Department 1988).

The following is an example of a model agreement currently being negotiated by the Union of Communication Workers on dealing with individuals suffering from stress.

Stress in the Post Office

1. The parties to this agreement recognise that stress at work is a health and safety problem and that employers have a duty under Section 2 of the Health and Safety at Work Act to take all reasonable practicable measures to prevent stress at work. Under Section 7 of the Act, employees have a duty not to endanger themselves or others and to co-operate with their employer in meeting statutory requirements.

2. This agreement will apply to all employees working in all areas of the Post Office Businesses' activities. The same opportunities for counselling and other help will be offered to all staff, regardless of sex, age, race, grade or job.

3. Where stress causes deterioration in job performance, this will be treated as a health problem and the sufferer will be encouraged to seek help under the terms of this policy. There will be no discrimination against individuals suffering from stress.

4. The organisation and arrangements for dealing with stress at work will form part of the employer's Health and Safety Policy, and should be read in conjunction with that policy.

5. Priority will be given to assessing the causes of stress at work and introducing measures to reduce or prevent stress. The Businesses will designate individuals, normally from the personnel function, who will be responsible for carrying out this assessment, in consultation with Union Representatives from the work area. Specific training will be provided for people carrying out assessment.

6. Counselling will be offered by trained counsellors who may be drawn from the Welfare Service. Such counselling will be strictly confidential between the counsellor and member of staff. No details or records will be disclosed without the written permission of the member of staff concerned.

7. Employees suffering from stress and stress-related illnesses will be offered paid time off to attend stress counselling sessions. In addition, names of stress counsellors and how to contact them will be posted on notice boards, so that staff can make arrangements for counselling outside their working hours if they wish. (This is for staff who do not want to ask for time off and draw attention to their need for counselling.)

8. Information and training will be given to all employees. This will include information on the causes and effects of stress; a copy of this stress agreement; arrangements for seeking help; arrangements for reporting causes of stress and work-related illnesses.

9. Employees unable to continue in their job because of stress-related illness will be offered alternative suitable posts, subject to agreed procedures for relocation. Relocation will be considered as a last resort, unless requested by the member of staff concerned.

10. This policy will be reviewed jointly by the POUC and the Post Office Businesses, on a regular basis. The initial review of effectiveness will take place twelve months after this policy comes into effect. Thereafter, reviews will be carried out at intervals of not more than two years.

Professor Cary Cooper of the University of Manchester Institute of Science and Technology said about an early study he had conducted: '*Stress counselling in the Post Office substantially reduced sickness absence and improved the mental well-being of employees. Although a structured cost benefit analysis was not undertaken, the reductions in sickness absence are likely to have produced substantial economic savings*'.

ASLEF, the train drivers' union, has also been successful in persuading management of the need to have in place a policy on dealing with workplace stress — in this case the stress caused by witnessing railway suicides, or other incidents where a person has been killed or seriously injured. In October 1992, the British Railways Board issued instructions for local managers aimed at reducing the risk of post-incident trauma for train crew involved with suicide, fatality or mear-miss incidents. The route managers' responsibilities include:

▲ making arrangements for the train crew to be interviewed as soon as possible to see whether they need to be relieved from duty.

▲ ensuring that the person, upon arrival at the home depot, is seen by a management representative for counselling.

▲ providing follow-up support and monitoring by a suitably qualified person, through home visits and telephone calls, to ensure continuing care, concern and support until the person returns to work.

▲ providing monitoring on return to work to establish whether further assistance is required. For all drivers, this includes ensuring that the person is accompanied in the driving cab on the first occasion they are required to work over the section of the route where the incident occurred.

▲ interviewing the person by a management representative again six weeks after the event to establish whether any further assistance/counselling is necessary.

In May 1994 an expansion of this policy was proposed by British Railways Board, to provide protection of earnings for workers taking time off following involvement in any serious incident.

NEGOTIATING A POLICY

Here are a few important points to think about in negotiating a policy for stress prevention.

1. **An agreed definition of stress**
   The first point in any agreement is to be clear about the terms of reference. There are many possible definitions. We have used the following: *When the demands and pressures placed on individual workers do not match the resources available, or do not meet the individual's needs and motivations, stress can occur and endanger that person's health and well-being. In the short term, stress can be debilitating; in the long term, stress can kill.*

2. **Company view of stress**
   It should be made clear in the initial paragraphs, that the company takes

the view that stress is a collective problem, that attempts will always be made to tackle the causes of stress and that individuals will not be victimised for reporting symptoms of stress and, on the contrary, will be offered assistance in the form of counselling, time off, etc.

It should be made clear that stress will be dealt with in a similar way to other hazards, according to the employers' legal duties under the Health and Safety at Work Act and the Management of Health and Safety at Work Regulations (see page 86).

3. **Agreed key factors which contribute to stress**
a) The Work Environment
Remember traditional workplace stressors like noise, vibration, chemicals, dust and other physical hazards such as lighting, ventilation, badly designed premises, machinery and equipment.

b) The Organisation of Work
Repetitive, monotonous work, too much/little work, shiftwork, hours of work, lack of autonomy or control over content pace/flow of work, including rest breaks. Meaningless or fragmented work. Lack of training, exclusion from decision-making affecting the individual and the work. Ambiguity of role.

c) Contractual factors
Lack of promotional opportunities, shiftwork, long or unsocial hours, job insecurity (temporary, short-term contracts, fear of redundancy), inadequate rest periods and holidays, low pay. Unpredictable hours or inflexible schedules.

d) Relationships
Bad relations with colleagues, supervisors; sexism, racism (including harassment and discrimination); customer/client complaints, risk of violence. Impersonal treatment at work, social or physical isolation. Low levels of support for problem solving and personal development.

4. **Agreed symptoms of occupational stress**
(See page 24 for list of symptoms)

5. Assessment

Duties under the HSW Act and the MHSW Regulations should be explicitly mentioned in the policy. There should be systematic identification of factors agreed to give rise to stress, environmental hazards, job design, organisational and contractual factors. This should be done through workplace inspections and audits, and through confidential surveys of perceived symptoms and causes of stress, preferably carried out by the trade union representatives.

6. Controlling risks

The focus should not be on counselling and training for workers without tackling organisational and job design changes. The focus should be on hazard control, including worker and trade union participation. So, for example, reviewing shift patterns, getting rid of or alleviating machine pacing; providing adequate instruction, supervision, information and training, with clear objectives and details of how those objectives are to be met. Improving the working environment to get rid of dust, chemicals, heat, cold, noise, vibration, heavy lifting, monotonous work and so on. Giving choice to workers over the selection of equipment and working and production methods.

7. Set up reporting systems

There must be clear procedures for workers to follow if they are suffering symptoms of stress, with the right to be represented at all times by their trade union. Reassurance must be given that individuals will not suffer discrimination or lack of status as a result of reporting symptoms of occupational stress. Counselling should be provided for those who wish to take advantage of it, and paid time off to recover should also be offered. A guarantee to investigate the causes of occupational stress must be given.

8. Information and training

Information and training about the causes and symptoms of occupational stress must be given to all employees, including copies of risk assessments and policy/procedures on stress. The trade union must be involved in the planning and provision of health and safety training and information, and should be given the opportunity to describe the role of the trade union in tackling hazards and representing members at work.

RECOMMENDATIONS ON MINIMISING EFFECTS OF SHIFTWORK AND NIGHTWORK

As we have shown in Part 2, shiftwork and nightwork are major contributors to workplace stress. Although results of recent research make concrete recommendations difficult, the following points need to be taken into account in constructing shift patterns with minimal effect:

▲ minimise permanent nights and limit the number of night shifts in succession (no more than two)

▲ the morning shift should not begin too early

▲ shift change times should allow individuals some flexibility

▲ the length of the shift should depend on the physical and mental load of the task, and the night shift should be shorter than the morning and afternoon shifts

▲ short intervals between two shifts should be avoided

▲ continuous shift systems should include some free weekends, with at least two successive full days off

▲ in continuous shift systems, a forward rotation is preferred, i.e workers should move from the morning to the afternoon to the night shift rather than rotate the other way

▲ the duration of the shift cycle should not be too long

▲ shift rotas should be regular

▲ rotas should be fixed well in advance and changes to rotas should be avoided.

AVOIDING EXCESSIVE WORK TIME

There is now a European Union Directive on working hours which accepts the basic premise that excessive work time is dangerous. The preamble to the Directive states:

▲ workers must be granted minimum daily, weekly and annual periods of rest and adequate breaks

▲ a maximum limit should be placed on weekly working hours

▲ the human body is more sensitive at night to environmental disturbances and certain forms of work organisation; long periods of nightwork can be detrimental to the health of workers and can endanger safety.

The Directive gives new legal rights to:

▲ a minimum daily rest period of 11 consecutive hours

▲ a rest break where the working day is longer than six hours

▲ a minimum uninterrupted rest period of 24 hours (in addition to the 11 hours' daily rest) every week — in principle this should include Sunday

▲ not to work more than 48 hours per week, on average (including overtime)

▲ paid annual leave of at least four weeks which is not replaced by an allowance in lieu where employment is terminated (three weeks for the first years the Directive is in force).

The British Government did all that it could to resist the introduction of the working time Directive which will come fully into force in the rest of the European Union in November 1996. The British Government has now decided to begin an action in the European Court over the Directive on the grounds that it was inappropriate to introduce it under the health and safety provisions of European law. The Government has announced that it will take no action at all to introduce the Directive until the court case is decided. This will have a special irony for those who are convinced that the Government has not properly implemented previous Directives but who have been deterred from going to the European Court by the delays and expense involved. The Government also secured a concession from its European partners. In the UK, there will be a further period of seven years during which workers can voluntarily work more 48 hours per week but cannot be forced to do so. Employers will have to fulfil specific conditions in such cases:

▲ the worker's agreement to perform the work must be obtained

▲ no-one must be subject to detriment if s/he does not agree to carry out such work

▲ the employer must keep up-to-date records of all workers carrying out such work

▲ the enforcement authorities must have access to these records and may prohibit or restrict the maximum weekly working hours on health and safety grounds

▲ the employer must provide the enforcement authority with information on cases where work exceeds the 48-hour limit.

The Directive does not apply to transport work, sea fishing and doctors in training. National governments have also the option of excluding other groups of workers and unions, and employers can devolve responsibilities for some parts of the Directive but not the maximum weekly working time.

Despite the limitations of the Directive, it offers opportunities as a bargaining weapon for trade unions. Unions were successful in obtaining reduced working hours agreements in the 1980s even if the ultimate effect was that those in full-time employment worked more overtime. There were notable strikes in the engineering industry in both Germany and the UK. Some unions are now looking to the Directive for further progress. MSF Assistant General Secretary Tim Webb, commenting on the aerospace industry, said, '*The provisions of the new directive will need to be incorporated in employees' contracts of employment. We need to protect our members' interests to ensure they are not pressurised to work excessive overtime. The aerospace industry is facing severe cutbacks and needs to plan ahead. Staffing levels and hours of work should be part of that plan.*'

The Directive also deals in some detail with nightwork:
▲ nightwork must not exceed an average of eight hours in any 24-hour period
▲ nightworkers whose work involves special hazards or heavy physical or mental strain must not work more than eight hours in any 24 hours during which they do nightwork
▲ nightworkers must have a free and confidential medical examination before they begin work and at regular intervals thereafter
▲ nightworkers with health problems connected with their work should be transferred wherever possible to suitable day work.

An 1990 report from the ILO goes further than the Directive in its recommendations on reducing the effects of nightwork (International Labour Office 1990). These are intended to cover all workers except those in agriculture and transport by water. The main provisions on working hours are:
▲ normal hours for nightwork should not exceed eight in any 24-hour period, except for work which only requires substantial periods of attendance or stand-by; the alternative work schedules should give workers at least equivalent protection over different periods of work
▲ hours of nightwork should generally be less and should never exceed those of the equivalent day work

▲ any improvements in working hours or holidays should accrue to nightworkers at least as much as day workers

▲ nightwork should be organised to avoid overtime as far as possible either before or after the shift; this proposal is strengthened further for hazardous or strenuous work

▲ where shiftwork involves nightwork, two consecutive shifts should not be performed and there should be at least an 11-hour rest period between shifts

▲ breaks to enable workers to rest and eat should be planned into the job, the frequency and length of these to be determined by the nature of the work.

The ILO Recommendation makes some specific points about health and safety:

▲ employers and workers' representatives should be able to consult occupational health services, where they exist, on the consequences of various forms of organisation of nightwork, especially when undertaken by rotating crews

▲ special attention should be paid to factors such as toxic substances, noise, vibration and lighting levels, and work involving heavy physical or mental strain — cumulative effects from such factors should be avoided or reduced

▲ the employer should take the necessary measures to provide the same level of protection against occupational hazards as for day workers, in particular avoiding as far as possible the insolation of workers.

A large number of supplementary measures are also proposed to reduce the stress of nightwork:

▲ the time spent travelling to and from work should be limited or reduced and safety when travelling should be improved in various ways, e.g. by co-ordinating work times with the schedules of public transport services, subsidising transport, provision of means of transport by the employer, assistance to workers in acquiring their own transport, the provision of accommodation within a reasonable distance of the workplace

▲ improvements should be made in the quality of rest of nightworkers, e.g. by advice and assistance of noise insulation of workers' homes

▲ suitable rest facilities should be provided at work

▲ suitable provision should be made for meals and drinks, including hot food
▲ creches or other services for the care of children should be available
▲ suitable cultural, sporting and recreational facilities should be provided
▲ nightworkers should be able to benefit from training and educational opportunities with paid leave
▲ pregnant women should be reassigned to day work
▲ the special situation of workers with family responsibilities, of workers undergoing training and of older workers should be taken into consideration when decisions are taken on the composition of night crews
▲ workers should be given reasonable notice of a requirement to perform nightwork
▲ arrangements should be in place for nightworkers to transfer to day work after a given period of employment
▲ long-term nightworkers should be given special consideration for voluntary early or phased retirement
▲ trade union representatives should have the same facilities as those on day work and should be able to carry out their functions under the conditions of nightworkers.

There is quite a large discrepancy between the law as defined in the working time Directive (quite apart from British wrecking efforts) and the ILO Recommendation. Nevertheless, the Recommendation does set out a bargaining agenda for trade unions who traditionally have been more interested in negotiating wage premiums than giving priority to the health and safety aspects of nightwork. The ILO makes clear that the effects on personal and social life are matters for collective bargaining to secure the best conditions and should not just be left to individuals to sort out for themselves.

RECOMMENDATIONS ON TACKLING VIOLENCE AT WORK

Employers' legal duties on preventing the risk of violence to their employees are the same as those outlined for prevention of stress in general, and indeed for any workplace hazard (see page 84). However, the following points of health and safety law are particularly important to highlight when considering policies on tackling violence at work.

▲ employers must provide safe systems of work (HSW Act, Section 2)

▲ co-employees must not pose risks to any other employee's health at work (HSW Act, Section 7)

▲ employers must conduct a suitable and sufficient assessment of the hazards to which their employees are exposed whilst at work (MHSW Regulations, Regulation 3)

▲ safety representatives have a legal right to investigate fully any incident of 'violence' occurring at work (SRSC Regulations, Regulation 4)

▲ HSE inspectors and environmental health officers, when they are responsible for a workplace, can:

1.) Enter any workplace to inspect and investigate

2.) By use of an improvement notice, order the employer to achieve employee protection

3.) By use of a prohibition notice, ban an employer from engaging in work that puts employees at risk

4.) Prosecute employers who fail in their legal duty.

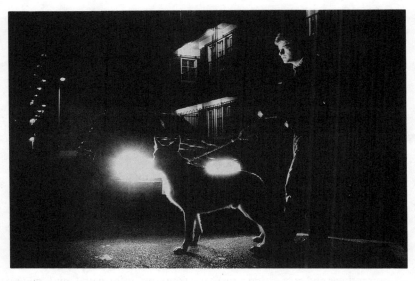

This security guard faces the stress of long hours, working alone and the nightly threat of violence.
Jez Coulson/INSIGHT

In 1992, the HSE served its first enforcement notice relating to violence on an employer when it ordered Rotherham Borough Council to reduce the risk of violence and make the working environment safe for its workers (*Bargaining Report* May 1994). The improvement notice followed campaining by the local government union NALGO (now part of UNISON) after a rent collector was killed on her rounds.

The response to violence, whether it is from members of the public or from colleagues and managers, is the same — violence at work is unacceptable and responsibility lies with employers, in consultation with workers, to:

a.) eliminate it,

b.) if unable to eliminate it, to reduce violence to the lowest possible level and, finally

c.) to protect employees from any residual risks.

Steps to take include:

▲ setting up a means by which employees can report and record all instances of violence or bullying

▲ employers must provide information, instruction and training on workplace procedures to a.) tackle violence and b.) to break down the perception that violence is an 'acceptable' feature of work

▲ reviewing safety policies to include sections on violence and bullying or, better, issuing separate guidelines or a code of practice

▲ including bullying as a disciplinary offence for all employees regardless of work status

▲ violence or bullying to be dealt with by grievance procedures where disciplining the perpetrator is not adequate.

▲ involving the HSE or local environmental health officer. Draft proposals to revise the Reporting of Injuries, Diseases and Dangerous Occurrences Regulations include a requirement to report to the HSE incidents resulting in employees being hospitalised or off work for three days or longer (Health and Safety Commission 1994)

▲ raising the issue in all union and joint union-management consultative committees and requesting a response (training, information and, where necessary, funding) from your union.

What to ask for

This list is not exhaustive but provides examples of things to aim for in negotiations on dealing with violence at work.

Changes in work practices

▲ improved levels of staffing
▲ provision of secure buildings or work areas
▲ withdrawal of service where risks are not tackled

Access to facilities and equipment

▲ provision of alarms, both personal and workstation based
▲ provision of protective equipment when appropriate
▲ safe transport at times of risk
▲ provision of portable communications equipment e.g. mobile phones

Changes in management practice

▲ setting up systems of incident recording
▲ making evaluations of incident records a standing item on safety committee agendas
▲ providing budget allocations for upgrading security measures
▲ assessing risks specifically to address violence from all sources
▲ developing, with worker consultation, violence policies that include regular policy evaluation and review
▲ using disciplinary measures to tackle abuse by supervisors
▲ providing regular training
▲ pursuing criminal prosecution of assailants.

Many unions have negotiated policies on dealing with violence at work. Despite its length, we are reproducing below in full the policy negotiated between UNISON and Oldham Metropolitan Borough in 1993 as an example of a comprehensive agreement based on the recognition by the Council that its employees are its most important resource, that violence and the risk of violence is a cause of workplace stress, and that employers have a responsibility to reduce the risk of violence to their employees.

Oldham Metropolitan Borough Code of Practice. Violence at Work. March 1993

The Council's Commitment

Through the introduction of a policy to address the increasing frequency of violence towards local government employees, the Council has committed itself to the objectives of reducing the risk of violence and to supporting employees who have been victims.

Oldham Metropolitan Borough is totally opposed to employees being at risk from violence at work. The Council considers its employees its most important resource and any complaint of violence at work will be treated seriously, and maximum help and support will be given to the victim.

This document has been written so that the policy on Violence at Work, and its implication, may be easily understood.

1. What is Violence at Work?

1.1   The Health and Safety Executive's definition of violence is: "Any incident in which an employee is abused, threatened or assaulted in circumstances arising out of the course of his or her employment".

1.2   Verbal abuse or threats are the most common forms of violence, but physical attacks are becoming more frequent.

1.3   The Council and Trades Unions recognise and accept that, locally and nationally, there is an increase in violence, and this policy addresses the problem.

1.4   The Council recognises the particular vulnerability of isolated and front-line workers, and believes that exposure to violence is not an acceptable part of their job. The Council also recongnises the specific vulnerability of women, ethnic minorities and people with disabilities. Violence includes not only physical attacks but threats and fear of violence, verbal abuse and harassment.

2. The Effects of Violence at Work

2.1   Both the employer and the employee have an interest in reducing the incidence of violence at work.

2.2   For the employee, violence can cause pain, disability and even death. More often, however, it causes anxiety and stress-induced illness. Any such damage to the health of employees is unacceptable, and the policy addresses this.

2.3   For the employer, violence at work can cause low morale, high absenteeism, high insurance rates and compensation costs.

2.4   Managers and Supervisors should be commited to reducing risks from violence. They should also support employees who have suffered violence. SUPPORT means providing an opportunity for the employee to share any feelings resulting from the incident with colleagues or outside counsellors as the need arises.

3. The Implications

3.1   All necessary steps must be taken to identify and eliminate the incidence of violence to employees during the course of their work. This involves developing the ability of employees to manage and deal with potential and actual violent situations.

3.2   In addition, the necessary support and appropriate remedies should be available to employees during and after violent situations. This includes access to non-departmental advisers and counsellors where requested.

3.3   There should also be, on a continuing basis, a development of policies and practices in respect of preventing violence against employees.

3.4   Finally, all departments need to increase awareness of the implications of potentially violent aspects of jobs. *This is to be done by paying attention to:*
job design, accommodation, management and supervision, work organisation, recruitment and selection, training. Such

awareness is a key component in reducing the incidence of violence.

4. Obligations, Rights and Responsibilities

4.1 It is the right of all employees to be at work in an environment which is as free as possible from the risk of violence.

4.2 It is also the right of all employees to expect management to take all possible steps to ensure the safety during the course of their work. Any known risks should be dealt with immediately.

4.3 In addition, in appropriate cases, employees should have the right to financial, legal and personal support in the event of them being the victims of violence arising out of the course of their work.

4.4 Employees should also have the right of access to the necessary and most appropriate form of counselling in the event of violence at work.

4.5 It is the responsibility of management to ensure the safety of all employees during the course of their work and to participate in the development of a support network of counsellors within the authority.

4.6 Departments will provide the names of volunteers who will be trained as counsellors and who will be available to provide support and advice to those who have been subjected to violence.

4.7 Departments will introduce an incident report book, similar to the existing accident report book, and record all incidents of violence.*

5. Complaints

5.1 Where there is a complaint of violence at work, it is understood that employees may well differ in their perception of the seriousness of the incident. Complaints should not be trivialised. They should be reported on the incident form.

5.2   Apart from asking for brief details, the form also asks for the events leading up to the incident, and the outcome in terms of damage or injury. There is also reference to any previous problem with the person involved; aggression can escalate over a series of meetings.

5.3   In addition, where actual bodily harm has occurred the statutory documentation must be completed. This is to protect the statutory rights of the injured employee.

6. Procedures

6.1   The Chief Officer of each department is responsible for the co-ordination of policy and practice in respect of violence at work.

6.2   Where an incident form is completed, a copy must be forwarded to the Personnel Department, who will be responsible for the overall co-ordination of policy.

6.3   Support, in the form of advice or counselling, should be available immediately, but it should be accepted that the victim may prefer this to come from someone outside the immediate work group. (A list of names will be provided.)

6.4   In certain cases, any appropriate financial, legal and personal support will be available to employees involved in violent indidents or harassment leading to criminal or civil proceedings.

7. Communication, Training and Monitoring

7.1   The policy will, through this document, be circulated to all existing employees. A summary of this will form part of the Recruitment Pack for any prospective employees. Posters and other publicity material will be circulated to all Council workplaces.

7.2   Corporate and departmental training programmes will be developed to increase awareness of violence as it affects people at work. This will include a definition of violence; how and why it can happen; an understanding of how even

> the threat of violence can cause tension, stress and sickness; and help to prevent violent incidents.
>
> 7.3   Training will also be given to identify areas of potential risk in work situations along with skills for coping with aggression and violence should it arise.
>
> 7.4   As part of the commitment under the violence at work policy, individuals will be identified across the authority to become counsellors. They will receive training in dealing with an initial response to victims of violence, including recognition of when to pass on a "client" to a professional, and also in the confidentiality aspects of such responses. A victim will be free to choose any such trained counsellor.
>
> 7.5   These procedures do not preclude victims from consulting their union representative. All the recognised unions have welcomed the initiatives of this policy, and are prepared to provide peer-group support to victims.

* The workplace accident book can be used to record *any* incident relating to workplace health and safety, including violence and the stress and other symptoms that may result.

EMPLOYERS' LEGAL DUTIES AND THE LAW ON STRESS AT WORK

Employers are required by law to do much more than provide counselling for individuals affected by stress-related illnesses. They have a duty to *prevent* and *control* workplace stress. A number of pieces of legislation are relevant:

Health and Safety at Work Act 1974

Employers have a general duty under Section 2 of this act to ensure the health, safety and welfare at work of all their employees. A responsibility for health includes mental health. The Health and Safety at Work Act also requires employers to provide safe equipment and working environments, safe methods of work and information, instruction and training. Inadequate provision of any of these can increase the risk of workplace stress. The inclusion of stress and mental health in the provisions of the Health and Safety at Work Act has been borne out by a recent Court of Appeal ruling that employers can be found negligent if they do not take steps to protect an employee's mental health from the results of overwork or stress *(Health and Safety Information Bulletin* October 1993).

Systems of work that give rise to the risk of stress are clearly not safe, and the employer therefore has a legal duty to make improvements, at least "as far as is reasonably practicable" to eliminate or adequately control the risk.

The phrase "so far as is reasonably practicable" means that employers can find a balance between the cost, time and trouble of making a job safe, and the likelihood of that job causing injury or illness.

Employers must make all improvements necessary to eliminate risks that they can foresee unless the cost of doing so grossly outweighs that risk. This process is known as **cost benefits analysis.** In order to make this process fair, an estimation must be made not just of the costs, but of the possible benefits of improved working conditions in terms of reduced sickness absence and staff turnover, avoiding claims for compensation and improved morale and productivity.

The law hinges firstly on a notional "reasonable employer"; secondly, on the foreseeability of risks according to available knowledge from, for example, HSE Guidance, trade press, views of staff and their representatives; and thirdly, the steps a reasonably prudent employer could be expected to take in the circumstances, bearing in mind the cost benefits analysis.

So, if problems are brought to the attention of management by staff or preferably by their trade union representatives, the employer is obliged to investigate the nature and extent of those problems, and to take steps to control or eliminate them.

In addition to the general duties in the Health and Safety at Work Act, employers now have to comply with the more specific provisions of recent UK legislation implementing several European directives.

Management of Health and Safety at Work (MHSW) Regulations 1992

The MHSW Regulations require employers to adopt modern risk management techniques.

Employers must:
- ▲ identify any hazards and make an assessment of all the risks to the health and safety of their employees, and record the findings of the assessment.
- ▲ review and modify risk assessments at regular intervals; when there have developments or changes in the work; if 'adverse events' have taken place (for example, workplace accidents or illness have occurred).
- ▲ apply the following principles or hierarchy to preventive and protective measures:
  a. avoid the risk altogether
  b. combat risks at source
  c. wherever possible, adapt work to the individual
  d. implement improved working methods and technological changes where these can make work safer
  e. incorporate risk prevention strategies as part of a coherent policy
  f. give a priority to those measures that protect the whole workplace
  g. provide workers with the means to understand what needs to be done to ensure safety
- ▲ provide health surveillance where the risk assessment shows that adverse health conditions have occurred or are likely to occur under the particular conditions of work.
- ▲ Employers *must* consult safety representatives in good time on any changes that may affect the health and safety of employees including the planning and provision of training.

The primary benefit of the health surveillance provision should be to detect adverse health effects at an early stage. In addition, it is a means of checking the effectiveness of control measures, providing feedback on the accuracy of the risk assessment, and identifying and protecting those who are at the greatest risk.

There needs to be a system for early detection of symptoms and rehabilitation in the context of a preventive strategy, aimed at identifying causes in every case. However, there must be some guarantees in place — workers cannot be expected to admit to health effects that may damage their employment prospects.

Regulation 6 obliges employers to appoint one or more competent persons to assist them in identifying and implementing the preventive and protective measures required. A competent person is described in the Regulations as being someone who has sufficient training and experience or knowledge and other qualities, and may be enlisted from outside the organisation or recruited from within it. Usually where a safety officer already exists, they will be the competent person, or the employer may wish to use consultants. However they decide to go about fulfilling this duty, the employer must consult the trade union safety representatives as to the appropriateness of the appointment and the adequacy of assessments and control measures. Although assessments are management duties, safety representatives may very well want to be involved in carrying them out, since they coincide with safety representatives' functions in carrying out inspections and monitoring management's compliance with relevant legislation. Representatives can provide invaluable information and expertise from the trade union on best practice.

Safety Representatives and Safety Committees Regulations 1978 (SRSC Regulations)

The principal mechanism for consultation and representation on health and safety in the workplace is provided by the SRSC Regulations. The SRSC Regulations were introduced under the HSW Act and have the same legal force at the Act itself. Where there is a recognised trade union, the members are legally entitled to elect at least one safety representative. Safety representatives have the right to inspect the workplace, get information held by the employer relating to health, safety or welfare, paid time off for training and to carry out their functions.

. Rail workers resist stress panels

Several years ago, traditional signal boxes in and around London were phased out, and control of overground train traffic switched to four main "power boxes".

Individual workers in each of the power boxes control a panel which regulates a section of the rail network. The panel includes rows of brightly coloured lights and other electronically displayed information. The rooms are lit by fluorescent lights. The work is highly responsible and demands extreme concentration and quick decision-making; if the planned route or timetable of one train changes it can affect the regulation of all the other trains being controlled by the panel worker. The work is organised around four overlapping eight-hour shifts covering 24 hours a day.

When panel regulation was first introduced, workers were expected to work an eight-hour shift on the panels, with only a 20-minute lunch break. Not surprisingly, the incidence of sickness absence caused by mental fatigue, headaches, eyestrain and even blackouts, was very high. The panels were renamed "stress panels" by the workers.

Fortunately for the panel workers, the RMT safety group, chaired by safety representative Raj Kumar, successfully negotiated an end to the one-break shift, and replacement by a work pattern including breaks of at least 20 minutes every two hours. Furthermore, during particularly busy rush hours, the agreement allows for the panels to be staffed by two, rather than one, workers.

As a direct result of these negotiations, by six months after the new work patterns were put into operation there was a drastic reduction in health problems.

This excellent example of the way in which safety representatives' action can protect the health of their members is now under threat from the privatisation process. However, with ample evidence of the effects on health of continuous stress panel working, RMT members will fiercely protect their negotiated right to regular breaks.

As Raj Kumar puts it: *'It makes no sense to force workers to operate the stress panels continuously — quite apart from the effect on workers' health, it costs British Rail far more in sick pay than they could gain by increased productivity. Furthermore, pushing workers to the limits of their endurance every shift would increase the risk of error, and subsequent delays and difficulties in regulating the rail network.'*

Safety representatives should:
▲ gather information from management. For example, any data on number and causes of death of employees, and data kept by management on sickness and from the accident book, as this may be useful in identifying patterns and in building up a case for positive action on stress.
▲ arrange meetings with other representatives and shop stewards to discuss strategies for collective bargaining on stress, as well as seeking support from the branch, regional office and union health and safety officer.
▲ distribute information on stress to members; organise meetings, ensure that everyone knows that stress is a trade union issue and how they can deal with complaints and concerns.
▲ conduct membership surveys or questionnaires of health symptoms and causes. Stress surveys are a vital tool to help involve other workers, build awareness and assemble evidence of the problem (see page 92 for a sample questionnaire).
▲ raise the issue, backed up by the information and the case you have established, at the safety committee and start negotiations with management.
▲ contact your local hazards centre for advice and support, and to contribute information to them.
▲ organise inspections to look at the workplace causes of stress.
▲ list the stressors in your workplace. From the list choose your priorities for action. Discuss these and propose strategies for dealing with the priority problems.

▲ use the results of the survey to prepare a leaflet for discussion with members on the stresses in your workplace. Note priorities and ideas for action.

▲ keep members informed at all times about progress.

Safety Committees

Regulation 9 of the SRSC Regulations states that where two or more safety representatives (not necessarily from the same trade union) ask the employer in writing to set up a joint management/trade union safety committee, they must do so within three months in consultation with the representatives. The committee must be balanced — management representatives must not outnumber trade union representatives.

Workplace (Health, Safety and Welfare) Regulations 1992

These regulations cover workplace conditions such as ventilation, temperature, lighting, cleanliness, space, and drinking, washing and rest facilities. As discussed previously, failure to provide and maintain these facilities can be a source of workplace stress. Regulation 25(4) specifically requires employers to provide suitable facilities for pregnant or breastfeeding women to rest. Regulation 25(3) requires the provision of rest facilities free of tobacco smoke for non-smokers.

Trade Union Reform and Employment Rights Act 1993 (TURER)

Although this legislation is intended to further weaken trade union rights, it contains a number of provisions that are important for those trying to improve workplace health and safety.

Section 28 provides protection for employees from victimisation because of health and safety activities and improved rights for pregnant women. Pregnant women who would otherwise have to be suspended from work on health and safety reasons have the right to be offered suitable alternative work or, if none is available, to be paid while suspended from work. Although, even after implementation of this Act, the UK still has some of the worst provisions in Europe for pregnant women, this clause should go some way to reducing the stress caused to pregnant women — and the consequent risk to health of women and their babies — of working in dangerous conditions.

Common law duty of care

Employers have a common law duty of care for their employees' physical and mental health. Employers may be found negligent if any employee develops a stress-related mental illness or condition as a result of a "reasonably forseeable" incident.

An employer's common law duty also operates as an implied term of the **contract of employment** *(Health and Safety Information Bulletin* June 1994). Any contract which imposes an absolute obligation on an employee to work an excessive number of hours on regular basis may be void under the Unfair Contract Terms Act 1977 as it may be regarded as an attempt by the employer to avoid liability for death or personal injury. There is a fundamental implied duty of mutual trust and confidence in every contract of employment. This duty may be breached as a result of serious or consistent abuse directed at an employee by the employer, or a failure by the employer to protect employees who are subject to abuse from other colleagues.

SURVEYS AND QUESTIONNAIRES

A fundamental activity in any plan to tackle workplace stress is the carrying out of a workplace survey or questionnaire. Surveys can vary in sophistication and scale. You may want to involve academics, in which you can either try to get local colleges/universities involved for free (try your nearest hazards centre for contacts and support), or get management to stump up cash for a consultancy. If you do want to enlist the help of outside "experts", make sure they are working with the trade union all the way, and that workers' confidentiality is ensured.

In the first instance, a trade union investigation is most appropriate. It is one of the first steps to raising the issue of stress formally with workers and management. You do not have to carry out a survey that would stand up to rigid tests of scientific validity; trade unionists do not have to be epidemiologists to establish from their membership that they experience work-related stress. A survey can be a means of conducting an initial investigation of the nature and extent of workplace stress.

However, you do have to do a lot of work to make sure the questionnaire is filled out by practically everyone. Obviously if only a small proportion of the workforce return the questionnaire you cannot use it as a basis for negotiations with management. So members must be actively encouraged to fill them in, hold meetings, circulate leaflets, help members fill in the questionnaires, make sure the context is clear — if they want something done about stress the onus is on the staff to demonstrate to management that there is a genuine problem. Make sure members know the survey is completely confidential.

A questionnaire will certainly increase members' awareness of occupational stress and it will provide valuable information for the trade union. You may consider it more appropriate to get the branch to undertake the survey, if it is a widespread problem. This would certainly help in ensuring anonymity, in pooling resources and in persuading management that stress is a genuine problem. It still means that the workplace representatives have to be prepared to do the legwork!

Model stress questionnaire

Stress results when demands made on individual workers are in excess of the resources to meet them. In order to provide convincing evidence that complaints of stress must be treated seriously and urgently, we are gathering information about the type and extent of stress in this workplace. Your answers to the following questions will be an important part of this information.

ANYTHING WRITTEN ON THIS QUESTIONNAIRE WILL BE TREATED WITH THE STRICTEST CONFIDENCE. YOU ARE NOT ASKED TO PROVIDE YOUR NAME.

Part I: Symptoms of occupational stress

1. *Do you suffer from any of the following?*

	Never	Sometimes	Often
headaches/migraine			
palpitations			
high blood pressure			
heart disease aches and pains			
sweating			
changes in appetite			
indigestion			
stomach ulcers			
asthma			
anxiety			
depression			
sleeplessness			
exhaustion			

2. *While working, do you ever feel*

	Never	Sometimes	Often
irritated			
angry			
frustrated			
helpless			
anxious			
confused			
depressed			
unable to concentrate			
bored			
apathetic			
over tired			

3. *How often do you use tobacco, alcohol or drugs to help with the above symptoms?*

	Never	Sometimes	Often
tobacco			
alcohol			
drugs			

Part 2: Causes of occupational stress

1. *Do any of the following apply to the conditions in your workplace?*

	Yes	No
not enough space		
no privacy		
isolated		
awkward layout		
too hot		
too cold		
noisy		

badly lit
unsafe
uncomfortable
inadequate rest facilities

2. *Is the equipment you use at work*

                                                   Yes   No

old
in poor condition
uncomfortable to use
often breaking down
badly sited
unsafe

3. *Assessments and inspections*
Have assessments been carried out on all hazards as required by the relevant legislation such as the Management of Health and Safety at Work Regulations, Control of Substances Hazardous to Health Regulations, Noise Regulations, Display Screen Equipment Regulations etc.?

Are hazards adequately controlled?

Have workers been consulted during the assessment process?

Are trade union inspections carried out?

4. *Do any of these factors apply to your work?*

                                                   Yes   No

little control over how job is done
excessive work load
excessive hours
boring
repetitive
underuse of your skills
lack of training for your work
staff shortages
poor shift arrangements
threats of violence
sexual harassment
racial harassment
poor management
inadequate worker consultation
no/poor childcare
no/poor facilities to allow for care of dependants
no/poor job security
low pay
privatisation
inadequate feedback
overbearing supervision
electronic monitoring

5. *What measures would you like to see to reduce stress levels?*

6. *Any other comments?*

We hope you find the information and ideas in this book useful and relevant in your workplace. In Part 4, we provide details of local hazards organisations, statutory bodies, and other contacts and resources that may also be of use in tackling stress in your workplace.

4

CONTACTS AND RESOURCES

HAZARDS CENTRES, WORK HAZARDS GROUPS AND TRADE UNION HEALTH AND SAFETY GROUPS

Birmingham Trades Council Work Hazards Committee, 8 Milk Street, Digbeth, Birmingham B5 5SU; Tel: 021-236 0801.

BRUSH (Birmingham Region Union Safety and Health) Campaign, Unit 304, The Argent Centre, 60 Frederick Street, Birmingham B1 3HS; Tel: 021 236 0801.

CAHIL (Campaign Against Hazards in London), 21 Theberton Street, London N1 0QY; Tel: 071 226 5436.

Devon Action on Safety and Health, 17 Waverley Avenue, Exeter, Devon EX4 4NL; Tel: 0392 52842.

Greater Manchester Hazards Centre, 23 New Mount Street, Manchester M4 4DE; Tel: 061 953 4037, EMail: MCRI:GM-HAZARDS.

HASAC (Health and Safety Advice Centre), Unit 304, The Argent Centre, 60 Frederick Street, Birmingham B1 3HS; Tel: 021 236 0801.

HASH (Hull Action on Safety and Health), 231 Boulevard, Hull HU3 3EQ; Tel: 0482 213496.

Health and Safety Project, Trade Union Studies Information Unit, 36 Bottle Bank, Gateshead NE8 2AR; Tel: 091 478 6611/88.

Keighley Trades Council Health and Safety Campaign, Keyhouse Project, Low Street, Keighley.

Liverpool TUC Health and Safety Committee and Trade Union Resource Centre, 24 Hardman Street, Liverpool L1 9AX; Tel: 051 709 3995.

London Hazards Centre, Headland House, 308 Gray's Inn Road, London WC1X 8DS; Tel: 071 837 5605; E-mail LONHAZ @MCR1.geomail.or/@gn: apc.org.

Lothian Trade Union and Community Resource Centre, 2a Picardy Place, Edinburgh EH1 3JT; Tel: 031 556 7318; EMail: GEO2:LOTHIAN-TUCRC.

Milton Keynes Health and Safety Group and Resource Centre, Labour Hall, Newport Road, New Bradwell, Milton Keynes Tel: 0908 606139.

Nottingham TUC Safety and Health Committee, c/o 118 Mansfield Road, Nottingham; Tel: 0602 281898.

Sheffield Area Trade Union Safety Committee, Mudford Buildings, 37 Exchange Street, Sheffield S2 5TR; Tel: 0742 753834.

South East Scotland Hazards Group, 10 Fountainhall Road, Edinburgh; Tel: 031 667 1081 x 3661.

South Hants Work Hazards Group, 55 Garstons close, Titchfield, Hampshire PO14 4EP; Tel: 0329 42932. E-Mail MIKE.MERRITT @MCR1.geomail. org.

Tyneside Hazards Group, 36 Bottle Bank, Gateshead NE8 2AR.

Walsall Action for Safety and Health, 7 Edinburgh Drive, Rushall, Walsall WS4 1HW; Tel: 0922 25860.

West Yorkshire Hazards Group, Box 22, Bradford Resource Centre, 31 Manor Row, Bradford BD1 4PS; Tel: 0274 725046.

Wolverhampton Hazards Group, 2/3 Bell Street, Wolverhampton; Tel: 021 236 0301.

Occupational health projects

Bradford Occupational Health Project, 23 Harrogate Road, Bradford, South Yorkshire BD2 3DY; Tel: 0274 626191.

Camden & Islington Occupational Health Project, St Pancras Hospital, 4 St Pancras Way, London NW1 0PE; Tel: 071 383 0997.

Leeds Occupational Health Project, Leeds Family Health, Brunswick Court, Bridge Street, Leeds LS2 7RJ Tel: 0532 450271 x 117.

Liverpool Occupational Health Project, National Bank Building, 24 Fenwick Street, Liverpool L2 7NE; Tel: 051 236 6608.

Sheffield Occupational Health Project, Mudford Buildings, 37 Exchange Street, Sheffield S2 5TR; Tel: 0742 755760.

Information about trade unions

Trades Union Congress (TUC), Congress House, Great Russell Street, London WC1B 3LS; Tel: 071 636 4030.

Scottish TUC, Middleton House, 16 Woodlands Terrace, Glasgow G3 6DF; Tel: 041 332 4946.

Wales TUC, Transport House, 1 Cathedral Road, Cardiff CF1 9SD; Tel: 0222 372345.

Irish Congress of Trade Unions, 19 Raglan Road, Dublin 4, Ireland; Tel: 0001 081 680641.

Irish Congress of Trade Unions, Northern Ireland Committee, 3 Wellington Park, Belfast BT9 6DJ; Tel: 0232 681726.

Information on local trade union organisations and on Trades Councils can be obtained from the Regional Councils of the TUC:

Northern, TUC Northern Regional Office, Swinburne House, Swinburne Street, Gateshead NE8 1AX; Tel: 091 490 0033.

Yorkshire and Humberside, TUC Regional Office, 30 York Place, Leeds LS1 2ED; Tel: 0532 429696.

North West, TUC Regional Office, Baird House, 41 Merton Road, Bootle, Merseyside L20 7AP; Tel: 051 922 5294.

West Midlands, TUC Regional Office, 10 Pershore Street, Birmingham B5 4HU; Tel: 021 622 2050.

East Midlands, TUC Regional Office, 61 Derby Road, Nottingham NG1 5BA; Tel: 0602 472444.

East Anglia, TUC Regional Office, 119 Newmarket Road, Cambridge CB5 8HA; Tel: 0223 66795.

South East, TUC Regional Office, Congress House, Great Russell Street, London WC1B 3LS; Tel: 071 636 4030.

South West, TUC Regional Office, 1 Henbury Road, Westbury-on-Trym, Bristol BS9 3HH; 0272 506425.

HEALTH AND SAFETY EXECUTIVE

HSE Information Centres

Contact the Sheffield Information Centre for details of your HSE area office.

Bootle Information Centre (personal callers only), St Hugh's House, Stanley Precinct, Bootle, Merseyside L20 3QY.

London Information Centre (personal callers only), Baynards House, 1 Chepstow Place, Westbourne Grove, London W2 4TF.

Sheffield Information Centre (phone and personal callers — the national public enquiry service is run from here), Broad Lane, Sheffield S3 7HQ; Tel: 0742 892345.

HSE BOOKS

HSE free leaflets and priced publications can be ordered from: HSE Books, PO Box 1999, Sudbury, Suffolk CO10 6FS; Tel: 0787 881165.

ENVIRONMENTAL HEALTH OFFICERS

Environmental health officers are employed by local authorities. Phone numbers will be in the Business and Services Directory or in the Thomson Local Directory.

FURTHER READING

General Information on hazards and health and safety

London Hazards Centre, *Daily Hazard*, Newsletter of the London Hazards Centre (four issues per year).

HAZLIT is the London Hazards Centre library database. For more information about on-line access, contact the London Hazards Centre.

Hazards, *Hazards Bulletin*, a magazine for safety representatives, (four issues per year).

Labour Research Department, *Labour Research* and *Bargaining Report*, LRD Publications, monthly magazines.

City Centre, *Safer Office Bulletin*, City Centre, (four issues per year).

Marianne Craig and Eileen Phillips, *Office Worker's Survival Handbook: Fighting health hazards in the office*, Women's Press, 1991, ISBN 0 7043 4201 4, £5.95

WHIN (Workers' Health International Newsletter), c/o Hazards, P O Box 199, Sheffield S1 1FQ. Covers the international hazards movement.

Further information on stress at work

All the major trade unions have produced some guidance on stress at work. Contact your union for details of their publications.

Labour Research Department, *Stress at Work — the trade union response.* (This useful 1988 pamphlet is currently being updated and a new version will be available in September 1994.)

MIND, *The MIND survey: Stress at work.*

Mental Health Foundation, *Mental Illness: The Fundamental Facts.*

Sutherland and Cooper, *Understanding stress: A psychological perspective for health*, Chapman and Hall.

Cooper, *No Hassle! Taking the stress out of work*, Century Books.

Yorkshire Television, *Dangerous Lives: The Stress Epidemic* (video).

Leeds Animation Workshop, *All Stressed Up* (video).

LONDON HAZARDS CENTRE PUBLICATIONS

VDU Work and the Hazards to Health, £6.50.

Protecting the Community — A worker's guide to health and safety in Europe, £9.95.

Basic Health and Safety: Workers' rights and how to win them, £6.00.

Sick Building Syndrome: Causes, effects and control, £4.50.

Toxic Treatments: Wood preservative hazards at work and in the home, £5.95.

Repetition Strain Injuries: Hidden harm from overuse, £6.00 (£3.00 to trade unions and community groups).

Fluorescent Lighting: A health hazard overhead, £5.00 (£2.00 to trade unions and community groups).

REFERENCES

AAOHN Journal (1991) 39 (9) 416.

Alfredson et al (1991) *International Journal of Epidemiology*, 22 (1) 57.

Bargaining Report (May 1994) Violence at Work, 139, 7-11.

Bramwell R and Davidson M (1990) *Office work and your health*, Inland Revenue Staff Federation.

British Medical Association (1992) *Stress and the Medical Profession.*

Burchell B (ed) (1994) *Social Change and the Experience of Unemployment*, Oxford University Press.

CBI (Conferderation of British Industry) (1993) *Working for your health — practical steps to improve the health of your business.*

Centre for Alternative Industrial and Technological Systems (1986) *Flexibility — Who Needs It?*

Civil and Public Services Association (1994) *Civil Service Motions for the 1994 CPSA Conference.*

Civil Service Occupational Health Service (1993) *Sickness Absence in the Civil Service*, Occupational Health Notice 93/3.

COHSE (1992) *Shiftwork and health. A negotiators' guide.*

COHSE (1993) *Tackling stress from health care work.*

Colie C F (1993) Preterm Labor and Delivery in Working Women, abstracted from *Seminars in Perinatology*, 17 (1) 37-44.

Cooper (1986) Job distress: Recent research and the emerging role of the clinical occupational psychologist. *Bulletin of the British Psychological Society*, 39, 325-331.

Cox (1993) *Stress Research and Stress Management: Putting theory to work*, HSE Contract Research Report No. 61/1993, HSE Books.

Davies and Teasdale (1994) *The costs to the British economy of work accidents and work-related ill health*, HSE Books.

Engineer (1993) 14 October 1993.

European Foundation for the Improvement of Living and Working Conditions (1991) *Guidelines for Shiftworkers*, Dublin.

European Commission (1992) *Europeans and Health and Safety at Work*.

Financial Times (4 January 1994).

GMB Journal (May 1994).

GMB (1993) *After Shock — A preliminary report into the levels of Post Traumatic Stress Disorder among Accident and Emergency Personnel of the London Ambulance Service*, Tristan Ravenscroft and GMB London Region, 28 January 1993.

GMB (1993) *Freedom to Kill — the case against deregulation*, 9.

Gold D R et al (1992) *American Journal of Public Health*, 82 (7) 1011.

Guardian (22 March 1994).

Harrington J M (1978) *Shiftwork and Health. A critical review of the literature*, HMSO.

Hazards (Summer 1993) Sick at Heart, 43, 5.

Hazards (Summer 1993) Consultation off the rails, 43, 11.

Hazards (Winter 1993/4) Boss talk, 45, 7.

Health and Safety Information Bulletin (April 1994) 220, 5.

Health and Safety Information Bulletin (June 1994) Occupational stress: management and the law, 222, 11-14.

Health and Safety Information Bulletin (October 1993) Employer's duty of care extends to mental health, 20.

Health and Safety Commission (1994) *Draft proposals for the Reporting of Injuries, Diseases and Dangerous Occurrences Regulations,* HSE Books.

Health and Safety Commission (1993) *Health and Safety Commission Annual Report 1992-3.*

Health and Safety at Work (September 1991) Interview with Sir John Cullen, Chairman of the Health and Safety Commission, 22.

Health and Safety at Work (July 1987) BT slammed over safety lapses, 7.

Health and Safety Commission (1994) *Review of Health and Safety Regulations — Summary of findings and of the Commission's response,* HSE.

Hygeia (1992) Stress in the Workplace, No.6.

Independent (20 January 1994) Employers face wave of RSI claims, 2.

Independent on Sunday (28 November 1993) Blue-collar workers suffer most stress.

Infante-Rivard et al (1993) Pregnancy loss and work schedule during pregnancy, *Epidemiology* 4 (1) 73-75.

International Labour Office (1992) *Preventing Stress at Work,* Conditions of Work Digest, Volume 11.

International Labour Office (1990) Recommendation 178 of the 1990 International Labour Conference.

Joffe et al (1986) *Buswork and Health — A comparison of one person operators, crew drivers and conductors,* TURC Publishing, Birmingham.

Karaki (1991) *Journal of Human Ergology* 20 (2) 137.

Kawakami et al (1992) Effects of perceived job stress on depressive symptoms in blue-collar workers of an electrical factory in Japan, abstracted from *Scandinavian Journal of Work, Environment and Health,* 18 (3) 195-200.

Labor Notes (1988) Detroit, USA, 19.

Labour Research (1994) February 1994, 14.

Labour Research Department (1988) *Stress at Work — The trade union response.*

Labour Research Department (1992) *Part-Time Workers — A Negotiators' Guide.*

Landsbergis et al (1993) Job stress and heart disease: Evidence and strategies for prevention, in *New Solutions,* 3 (4) 42-58.

Melamed et al (1992) Noise exposure, noise annoyance and their relation to psychological distress, accident and sickness absence among blue collar workers — the Cordis Study, abstracted from *Israel Journal of Medical Sciences,* 28 (8-9) 629-635.

Moore-Ede M (1993) *The 24 Hour Society — The risks, costs and challenges of a world that never stops,* Judy Piatkus (Publishers) Ltd.

NASUWT (1994) Motion (9) passed at NASUWT 1994 Annual Conference.

National Group on Homeworking (1990) *The National Homeworker.*

Observer (10 April 1994).

Rochez and Scoggins (1993) Stress out, cash in. In *DAC Reports,* Davies Arnold Cooper Solicitors.

Rosa R R and Colligan M J (1992) *Experimental and Occupational Medicine*, 2nd edition, Little, Brown Publishers, 1173.

The Safety and Health Practitioner (May 1992) Shiftwork and Health, 18.

Travers C and Cooper C (1993) Mental health, job satisfaction and occupational stress among UK teachers, *Work & Stress*, 7 (3) 203-219.

TUC (1993) *Stress at Work — Initial Report*, TUC Health and Safety Project, Common Action Priority Team.

Waterhouse et al (1990) *Shiftwork, health and safety. An overview of the scientific literature 1978-1990*, HMSO.

Wedderburn A (1994) *Shiftwork, Health and Personality Hardiness. An apparent double link*, Heriot-Watt University, Edinburgh.

Zenz C (1988) *Occupational Medicine: Principles and practical application*, Year Book Medical Publishers, London, 1087.

INDEX